"In *Live Sent*, Jason Dukes is communicating a message that is vital for people to truly understand the mission for which they were created. *Live Sent* is vital for pastors if they are truly going to lead missional churches."

—Ed Stetzer, church planter, author, www.edstetzer.com

"Jason Dukes is the real deal—a living letter, sent into the world(s) that God has called him to. Here he articulates an intensely practical, decidedly missional, philosophy of life in a way that anyone can access. A blessing."

—Alan Hirsch, author, *The Forgotten Ways*

"Jason Dukes not only unpacks and teaches living sent in this book, he models it as a follower of Jesus, husband, dad, son, pastor, and friend. *Live Sent* is an amazing book that has made a radical impact on my life and the life of our church family in New Orleans. Thanks, Jason, for this gift and thanks for being a great mentor in my life."

—Rob Wilton, pastor, Vintage Church, New Orleans, Louisiana

"Great book! I've seen you and your posse live out what you believe."

—Brent Foulke, director of special services, Stadia East

"Some lessons can be learned from a textbook, others from a conference or podcast. But when my friend Jason Dukes began to explore all that is involved in the word missional, he chose the laboratory as the best learning environment. And that laboratory was and is a new church God planted through him. *Live Sent* is a report of lessons learned in that lab. Jason comprehensively negotiates the many aspects of church as missional—things like the gathering, intimacy with our Father, hindrances to living sent, etc. This book is filled with good research and inspiring stories!"

—Randy Millwood, coach/consultant, leadership development, spiritual transformation, small-group ministry, Baptist Convention of Maryland/Delaware

"As Jason Dukes shares his views on living sent by loving others, it is clear that he speaks from his heart. For the first time in my life I actually get that I don't simply go to church, but I am the church and my mission in life is to love and serve others. *Live Sent* shows you how to walk the talk of giving yourself away to others in every aspect of your life. Jason and his wife, ...

—Julie

Other New Hope books by Jason C. Dukes

Cartas Vivas (Spanish-language *Live Sent*)

*beyond MY church (*releasing January 2012)

LIVE SENT
you are a letter

2 CORINTHIANS 3:3
RD
3 AUG
2009

1, 1, John, 20:21

USA 13

jason c. dukes

NEW HOPE
PUBLISHERS

Birmingham, Alabama

New Hope® Publishers
P. O. Box 12065
Birmingham, AL 35202-2065
www.newhopepublishers.com
New Hope Publishers is a division of WMU®.

Library of Congress Cataloging-in-Publication Data

Dukes, Jason C.
  Live sent : you are a letter / Jason C. Dukes.
     p. cm.
  ISBN 978-1-59669-315-9 (sc)
  1. Christian life. I. Title. II. Title: You are a letter.
  BV4501.3.D84 2011
  248.4--dc22
                                2010053988

ISBN-10: 1-59669-315-0
ISBN-13: 978-1-59669-315-9

N114149 • 0411 • 7.5M1

Cover and book design: Michel Lê

for my mom
(thankful for the letter you were)

contents

0

an introduction

(you are a letter)

You are a letter. An email. A message. Your everyday life is more than just a story being written. Your very life is a letter. You were created to receive and send a message intentionally into the lives of the people you do life with daily.

Simply stated, you were made to know life abundantly, and life abundant happens when you live beyond yourself. No longer is it enough to ask the question, What am I supposed to do with my life? In fact, "no longer" is not appropriate. Your life was never intended to just be about you. It's never enough to simply ask questions about you, with regard to what you are supposed to do or what you want most to do.

A better question would be this: What's my part in this epic called humanity? The people whom you encounter every day actually need you. They need you, and you need them. We all need each other—to know each other. And, our lives both complement and supplement one another.

That's how humanity works. Together. I am shortchanged, in fact, when you are not all you were intended to be in relationship with me. You are shortchanged when I am not all I was intended to be in relationship with you. It could be said that I don't love you if I don't deliver into your life the message written in me and through me.

That's how love is demonstrated and how relationships happen and how people find abundant life as they were intended to find it.

The Sender (God) delivered His message to us and then writes His message in us and through us for us to deliver to others. He sends us. We are His letter of love into the culture around us to the people whom He loved enough to die for. He asks us now to love in the same way.

[God has always been sending a message]

In the Garden, His message was obvious. He loves us and made us to know His love and walk with Him.

To Noah, His message was a bit more emphatic. People had become so selfish. They no longer were even thinking of God, remembering that He made them. So, He cleansed the earth with a torrential rain. Those who believed His message remained.

To Abraham, His message was very moving. Literally. He told him to follow Him to a place that He would show Abraham. God was establishing a people who would both hear His message and be His message unto all the world.

To Moses, His message of compassion burned with passion, communicated through a bush on fire that was not consumed. God had heard the cries of His people from Egypt. He longed for them to cry out for Him in all times, not just times of trouble or for some favor from Him. Nonetheless, He intended to rescue them before they cried out, before they were trapped in themselves. He told Moses to go and rescue them. He sent Moses, but with a message that this was just temporary rescue. The ultimate Rescuer would ultimately come.

Through the prophets, His message was more direct, but still loving. Trumping the beliefs that God was cold and distant, He came near through the prophets' messages. He told those to whom the prophets spoke how much He hated all of their religious show. That's not why He made them. He didn't make them so that they could protect their image, but so that they could live in His image. To love. To know. To be. The I AM desired for them to be in complete life connection with Him. The prophets repeated something Moses said. They exclaimed that the ultimate Rescuer was coming. The One whom God would send, they were to trust Him. Follow Him. He would be the ultimate message of God's love.

And then the One who was sent, came. Jesus.

Jesus said in the Gospel of John, "As the Father has sent me, so I am sending you" (John 20:21). In fact, *sentness* is a theme throughout the stories of Jesus that are found in the New Testament of the Bible. He emphasized how He was sent with a message. John even called Him the Word—an ultimate message or complete communication from God. Just the fact that

introduction

God would put on human skin and walk among us, be Emmanuel, indicates how important sentness is to God. The message would continue.

Paul attempted to explain the teachings of Jesus further, introducing a very picturesque and challenging metaphor in 2 Corinthians 3. There, he defended the focus, authenticity, and credibility of the message he delivered and the ministry he lived. He said that the people who received from him this message of Jesus were now letters written by the Spirit of the living God. Their very lives were a message that God penned without a pen. He etched it into their lives.

The message continues to be sent today. The Sender continues to write His message as He always has. Better said, He does more than write or type it. He embeds it. Not on tablets, but on our hearts.

And so, you are a letter. I am a letter. If we follow Him, He continues to write His message in our hearts and through our lives. And, we live sent as a letter from God to culture, sharing the same message He has been delivering all along: I love you. I am near. Follow Me.

[the message of this book]

For more than seven years now, our church family, Westpoint Church, has been emphasizing the message and mission of living sent. During that time, several people who mentor me and speak encouragement into my life challenged me to write this book about this emphasis. For introduction's sake, here are four elements I would suggest are of utmost importance to the mission of being the letters that we were intended to be as followers of Jesus. The content of the chapters that follow simply unpacks these four elements.

First, in order to live sent, there may be some things we need to rethink. Foundational stuff. Life. Church. Relationships. Intention. Some thoughts and questions are shared on this foundational stuff in the first part of the book.

Second, living sent is all about trusting your value. The primary hindrance for a follower of Christ who is made to live sent is that he or she does not trust his or her God-given value. What we need to understand is that our value is not appraised—it is declared. Trusting what God has declared about us and that He has entrusted His message to us for delivery is crucial to being the letter He made us to be.

Next, living sent is all about doing life together. The epic of humanity, as I mentioned earlier, should be seen most beautifully within the movement Jesus started that He called His "church." Unfortunately, this is too often not the case. We tend to just be letters to each other and miss the importance of being letters into culture. Or, we are such vicious letters to one another that the culture around us would not read us anyway. They want to find love, and they often don't see it lived out among the church. So, how can we begin to do life together as humanity as we were made to do life together? Some suggestions are offered herein.

Finally, living sent is all about giving ourselves away intentionally. Jesus gave Himself away with restorative intent. We know what love is in that Jesus gave up His life for us, so we should give up our lives for others (1 John 3:16). It's one thing to serve only because of obligation or personal satisfaction. It's one thing to serve because of how it makes me feel. It's another altogether to serve in love for the sake of what happens in the life of the ones we serve. We must love—and show that love by serving—so that love and life are given into and brought out of others. I will share some stories and thoughts later in the book about this too.

My prayer is simply this—that you will find your true self, your created-by-God, sent-by-God, love-because-He-first-loved-us self, and that the church will be released to be the letters from God that He has written them to be.

[sharing stories . . .]

*A*t the beginning of each chapter, a story of living sent will be shared. I think it is important to share these stories for two reasons. First, I hope it will give you the chance to see that living sent matters. Lives have been changed and are being changed. Hurts are being healed. Loneliness is being transformed into togetherness. Brokenness is being restored. Secondly, I hope you will read these stories and think, I can do that. Because you can. It's not complicated. You were made for it.

[I challenge you]

If you follow Jesus already, I challenge you to enter into this conversation with an open heart and mind. I am sharing some thoughts that I have learned and continue to learn. In doing so, I am surrendering some thoughts that I had learned and needed to unlearn. You may need to do that too.

If you don't dig the religious thing or if you see Christians as arrogant and judgmental, keep reading. I assure you, what is often seen in the media about people who call themselves Christians is not what Jesus intended for His followers. What gets the most press, unfortunately, is not what He wanted when He asked His followers to be "salt and light" in this world. God may be calling you to be an agent of change and influence and, most importantly, of love and restoration.

Remember, God has always been sending a message. Are you His letter carrying His message as He intended you to be? Is your life a letter of His love? Maybe you and I need to listen again to what Jesus taught, rethink some stuff, and allow the Author to rewrite the motive and focus of our lives.

The Sender has sent you and me to be His letter of love unto humanity. May we live sent daily. And may we begin now.

[CONSIDER and CONVERSE]

At the end of each chapter, you will find a section called "Consider and Converse." These are simply questions for you as you continue to process what it means to live sent. Use them for personal reflection. Use them for small-group discussion. Use them to put your dog to sleep at night. Regardless, they are there to help you as you journey on in this ongoing conversation of life. Here they are for "chapter 0."

[1]   Why not ask the question, What am I supposed to do with my life?

[2]   The book begins with the statement: You are a letter. In view of a relationship with God, how might you explain this statement to someone?

[3] Can you find any examples of God sending His people and His message in the Bible?

[4] Based upon the four elements of this book, discuss the following questions:

- What does the church (as a body of believers) need to rethink?
- What does the church need to trust?
- What is the church made to do?
- What should the church give up?

1

Rethinking your "live"

(the bulk mail called humanity)

[a story_Catalina]

Catalina first discovered our local church family at a Fourth of July picnic in 2004. She was living in a different city at the time, but her brother had just moved into the community where the party was. She didn't personally connect with any of the people from our church family that day, but she remembers an announcement about when and where the church gathered. Something about what she saw and heard that day sparked an interest deep down inside of her. That was our first connection.

Quite unexpectedly, as God would have it, she ended up getting a promotion and transferring to a bank branch near where our church family gathered. It happened to be the bank where we would soon open our accounts.

We met Catalina when we officially opened an account there at that bank. She remembered the Fourth of July picnic and connected us with that church family she had heard about there. We invited her to our Sunday gathering, but she later recalled, "It took me a while to build up the courage to go, because I was by myself."

About a month later, she showed up to "try" our Sunday gathering. She remembered later how genuinely loving and interested in getting to know her everyone seemed to be. She told me she had never felt anything like that "in a church" before. That was a second connection.

At that gathering, one of our ladies invited Catalina to come to be a part of a ladies' group. She was invited again at the bank, when we went in to make a deposit. Catalina was longing for friendship, and being new to the area, she decided to go. She loved the way the ladies made her feel, like she belonged even though they hardly knew her. That was the third connection. And fourth and fifth and so on, because she connected with more than one woman that night.

Over time, she began to do more than spectate. She began to participate.

And the conversations she participated in and the times that they would discuss the Bible and the life they did together stirred up something in her heart. She had been exposed to forms of Christian religion growing up, but in this group of ladies she saw the love of Jesus alive and radiant.

Parts of her personal life would have bothered certain "churchgoers," but no one scolded her. Those ladies loved on her, accepted her where she was, and without compromising anything allowed God's Spirit to speak to her heart. And He did. She was reading His letters of love in the lives of those ladies who included her and who were living sent right before her eyes.

She began attending our gathering. She stayed faithful, doing life with those ladies. And then one night, she came over to the house for dessert with my wife and me. She said she was appreciative of how our church family made her feel like she belonged. It was about all of these people living sent together. The church alive 168 hours of the week.

She recalls it this way: "I felt the way I did when I went to the first gathering. I say all of this to show how consistent you all were at planting seeds and watering them, without ever imposing."

She said she had seen Jesus' love and was following Him now, in a relationship with Him like never before. She said she felt in her heart that some parts of her personal life were not what God wanted for her. She knew it would not be easy, but she wanted to make a change. She wanted God to be the love of her life and change her from the inside out and sustain her. Imagine that. We didn't judge her. We loved her. And God's Spirit spoke into her life and transformed her.

She read God's letter at the bank and in her neighborhood among those ladies. It took time. Like over 15 months. She saw His kindness and His message firsthand. Now she's a letter, too, living sent to her neighbors and in the marketplace.

[the bulk mail called humanity]

*L*ike it or not, we live in the bulk mail called humanity. Personally, I like it a lot. Why? Because I like to people-watch. It gets tough, though, when I have to pause a moment to watch me, to examine my motives, to rethink my "live." What do I mean by that? To live sent involves both "live" and "sent." Our sentness will always be determined by our "live." Better said, our mission will always be determined by who or what it is we live for.

Every day, we choose who or what we live our lives for. We choose our mission. Jesus phrased it this way: "If any of you wants to be my follower, you must turn from your selfish ways, take up your cross daily, and follow me" (Luke 9:23 NLT). He clearly emphasized that we either will live for ourselves and our personal pursuits, or we will live surrendered to Him and committed to the mission He intended for us. I live for myself, or I live for God. And it's been that way forever.

The real choice that Adam and Eve made in the Garden was this: live like God knows best or like Adam and Eve knew better. What else could they have wanted? I guess they didn't know how good they had it. Until they ate of the tree of All Knowing. Then they knew more than they probably wished they knew.

God's commands to us are so practical. In the case of the Garden, He must not have wanted them to eat of the fruit of the tree of All Knowing so that they would not know how fully capable they were of losing their "live." God told them to eat of the tree of the Fruit of Life all they wanted. Why? Because He made them to experience His gift of love and life. And what a life they had!

Complete freedom! Freedom to walk with God face-to-face. Freedom to be with one another unhindered by materialism and insecurity (naked as jaybirds they were!). Freedom to hang out with Simba the lion and Baloo the bear all they wanted. Freedom to enjoy all that God made rather than toil over all that God made.

Like I said, God's commands are so practical. He told them not to eat of the tree so that they would not "know" anything but life. "Evil" always tries to steal our "live." Tries to turn us inward, convince us we know better, move us toward giving up life as we were made to live it. This would be a good definition for evil, I think—being anything other than what we were intended to be.

Did you notice that "evil" is "live" spelled backward? It is interesting, because evil is living in an opposite direction from what we were created to live. Remember, we are thinking about this philosophically. There's a point coming soon.

So, God did not intend His most precious element of creation to know anything but life. He never intended them to know death. They chose to know how fully capable of being evil they were. They chose to know something other than what God meant for them. They chose to know when they ate of the tree of All Knowing, and humanity has regretted it and questioned it ever since.

They made a choice for all of us really, since the consequence of their choosing life as they wanted it separated them and us from the Life-Giver Himself. Their consequence has shown itself in the self-absorption so clearly demonstrated throughout our world. Their consequence actually was death (separation from the Life-Source), and we have all seen and felt its sting in so many ways.

God wasn't caught off guard by this, though. Did you know that? The Scriptures say that even before He made us, He knew He would reap upon Himself what was sown in the Garden. He would fix a problem He didn't cause. He would restore a relationship He didn't betray. He would die a death He didn't deserve.

In fact, He would use it to set the stage for the most demonstrative expression of His love. That's why the sacrificial system was introduced in the Old Testament of the Bible, and why it was brought to completion in Jesus. Because the consequence of death wasn't something *the created* could reverse. It was something only *the Creator* could reverse. And He did, in the fullness of time.

At the right moment of history, God would put on human skin. Jesus entered a culture steered by a self-righteous group of Jewish religious leaders who were both manipulating and being manipulated by a controlling but appeasing Roman government. It was that tension that would force their hands to kill any revolutionary who dared speak against the establishment, who dared call out the motives of leaders who were not carrying out a God-given mission as the Life-Giver intended. As people became more enthralled with Jesus' insightful teachings and were wowed by His growing popularity, the balance of power was threatened. This threat could possibly bring down a mighty blow from the Roman authorities that were permissive of Jewish practices in this Jewish province, as long as there was nothing that would call attention to the special treatment they were getting.

Jesus called attention to it. To their selfishness and greed and power-hunger. To how they were leading people astray. Exploiting people for personal gain even. And they wanted Him dead.

So, in an astonishing act of love, He let them kill Him. He prayed a prayer on that cross that spanned actions all the way back to the Garden and all the way to the end of time. He asked His Father to forgive them, declaring that they did not fully know what they were doing. They did not know as much as they thought they knew, and they did not know the depth of the love displayed right before their eyes. "But God demonstrates his own love for us in this: While we were still sinners, Christ died for us" (Romans 5:8). The ultimate expression of His love—taking the reaping of death upon Himself, and abolishing it as a forever consequence, restoring us to Garden-like relationship with God, all at the same time.

What love is this! And what better time and place to do it. What an amazing season of history. A time and place when one 20-by-90-mile piece of property called Israel was a land bridge connecting three continents. A time and place when a festival was in full swing, and many people from many places had gathered in that one spot for the festival. A time and place when those gathered were capable of taking an astounding message of love back with them in rapid fashion into the whole world, due to an amazing road system implemented by a forward-thinking Roman government.

Before He spoke time into existence, God planned to step into it to restore a relationship that we put into disrepair. In the fullness of time, He came.

(Galatians 4:4)

Here's the point: He made us to know Him and to give us His love. So, His ultimate mission was to choose to live beyond self. To give love. To not just live for self. That choice is not seen any better than in the way He showed us how to live, in the way He showed us how to choose who or what we would live for.

Paul wrote in Philippians 2 that Jesus did not regard being equal with God as something to hold tightly to. Instead, He set it down to put on skin, to become human, to walk among us, and to die a shameful death. All so that we could know life again instead of what we came to know in the Garden, when Adam and Eve ate of the fruit of the tree of All Knowing and took on a burden God never intended for them. Even after Adam and Eve's betrayal of the instructions from the One who knew best how they could best live, God Himself bore the fruit of their choice upon Himself. He loved, even in unlovable circumstances, a people who did not necessarily reciprocate His love. He now calls us to choose to love others in the same way.

He wants us to rethink our live so that we love God and love people first. So that we embrace our God-given mission instead of our self-absorbed pursuits. So that we let go of the things we hold tightly to because we think we deserve them. So that we give our lives away as life has been given to us.

So what, right? All this philosophical stuff sounds great, but how does it change the way I live every day? Here are some suggestions for everyday practices that we may need to rethink in light of God's intentions for us and in light of His intentional love.

[right and wrong]

If we rethink our live and embrace wholeheartedly a life lived beyond ourselves rooted in the ways of Jesus, then it will change how we define right and wrong.

Have you ever stopped and thought about this? We tend to even be selfish in the ways we think of right and wrong. We tend to think of them on a personal level rather than on a humanity level. Before you discount me as some misguided weirdo, hear me out.

In challenging His hearers to rethink their live, Jesus told a story about a true neighbor. You may have heard it called the parable of the good Samaritan. It's found in Luke 10. A guy was robbed and left for dead. Three people came along. The first was a priest. He did nothing. The second was a Levite. He did nothing. The third was a Samaritan. He helped the man.

I have heard teachers teach that story many times. For the most part, they have said that it is about a man (the Samaritan) who does what was not expected of Him (because Jews and Samaritans were bitter neighbors), while two holy people (both of a priestly nature) who should have cared about the man, didn't do a thing. Nothing wrong with that approach. Definitely true to the story. Here's a different angle.

Let's not forget the original question posed to Jesus. An expert in the law, in right and wrong, approached Jesus. He asked Him, "What do I need to do to get eternal life?" Jesus answered with a question, "What's written in God's law?" Pretty good question for an expert of the law. The man responded, basically saying to love God and love your neighbor. Jesus told him to do this, and he would live. Pretty simple.

So, the expert of the law asked the real Expert of the law if there might be a time when love for God and love for people might conflict. In other words, God might want me to do something found in the law that would prohibit me from having to show love to someone. It's quite possible, based on the characters of the story with which Jesus responded, that the motive of the man was very selfish. He was looking for a loophole of sorts, because there were people he really didn't want to show love to, like Samaritans.

Jesus answered with the story of the good Samaritan. What is obvious from the story is that the man whom the Jews despised helped out a Jew when even the Jews themselves didn't help. Looking deeper, maybe we should give the priest and Levite a break. They were only doing what was written in the law for them to do. They were avoiding a man left for dead whom they thought was dead. According to the law, that man, if he was dead, was unclean. They were not to touch him. So, they passed on by. How would they have known if he was Samaritan or Jewish, as beaten up as he was? They did the right thing according to the law they knew.

What Jesus really seemed to be saying was this—while you guys (the so-called law experts) are spending so much time trying to find loopholes in your lists of do's and don'ts, there is an entire nation of people *who happen to be your neighbors* (nationally speaking) whom you despise. The ones you despise understand "love your neighbor" better than you do. Quit looking for a concept of right and wrong in your ever-expanding lists of rules, and try determining right and wrong based on the very foundational commandment you claim to live by—*love God and love your neighbor*. Quit knowing your law so well, and get to know Me.

So Jesus closed the interaction, asking the man which person was a neighbor. The so-called expert in the law answered, probably begrudgingly, the Samaritan. Jesus said, "You go and do the same."

On another occasion, Jesus was asked what the most important of God's commands are. He answered again with "love God and love your neighbor." In fact, He concluded the answer with this statement, "These two commands are pegs; everything in God's Law and the Prophets hangs from them" (Matthew 22:40 *The Message*).

If this is the case, then isn't it safe to say that what is right and what is wrong, what is abiding by God's law and what is not, could be discerned with a simple question? Here's the question:

> In this choice I have to make, what should I choose to do, so that God knows I love Him, and the people involved and impacted know that I love them too?

Remember, I said we even tend to be selfish in the way we think of right and wrong. We think of it on such a personal level. We think of it in terms of whether we are right or wrong, rather than in terms of whether we are doing people right or wrong by our choices. Whether we are loving them or thinking only of ourselves. Whether we are thinking about the impact of our choices on just ourselves or on all of humanity.

This has very practical implications in how we rethink our live and how we make choices in daily life. All of a sudden, the Ten Commandments make sense as practical commands for living rather than just a list of what to do or not do. If you need to refresh yourself as to what they are, you can find them in Exodus 20 of the Old Testament.

Think of them in this way, practically. If I love God, I won't betray our relationship and give my worship to someone or something else. If I love someone, I won't steal from him. If I love my neighbor, I won't covet his stuff. If I love my spouse, I won't give my love to another in adultery. If I love my friend, I won't lie.

Let's take it into the marketplace. If I love my boss and co-workers, I will work hard so as not to get in the way of the progress of the team. If I love my boss and co-workers, I will not cheat them or talk about them behind their backs at all, but especially not for personal gain.

Take it to whatever application you want. People say that right and wrong can sometimes be black and white and that sometimes there are gray areas. When you think of right and wrong based on the pegs of "love God and love people," black and white and gray become beautiful colors of intimate relationship and abundant life when the right choice is made, but they become dark loneliness and spiraling self-destruction when the wrong choice is made. Gray is done away with. This principle of love can be applied in all situations because love is foundational in all situations. It's how we were made. It's no longer about being black or white, but rather being loving or selfish, connecting or disconnecting relationship.

[defining success]

*A*nother practical implication is this: If we rethink our live and embrace wholeheartedly a life lived beyond ourselves rooted in the ways of Jesus, then it will influence the way we define success in life. Is success for you defined by personal accomplishment or by other people's advancement? Are the people around you advancing because of how you've given your life away to them? Is success for you defined by personal checklists or changed lives?

Take a minute to read Matthew 25:31–46. How is success defined here? Like the goats, some of us focus on keeping score, defining ourselves by checklists. We make note of when we care for someone. However, like the sheep, some of us are able to look beyond checklists and end up changing lives without noticing. The fruit from this group is evidenced by the fact that, when the Master thanked them for what they had done, they asked, "When did we do that?"

Jesus spoke of success in terms of fruit. In other words, in terms of what blossoms out of our lives, springing into life around us. He spoke of success as what was caused by our living, rather than what we gained from our own pursuits in life. Other people's lives blossoming would be the evidence of true love poured out and sincere friendship lived out. It would be a demonstration that we have rethought our live to be Christ-centered and others-centered rather than self-absorbed.

People tend to have a "win at all cost" definition of success. Jesus had a "lose to win" values system—lose your life to gain life (Luke 9:24). For Him, success was defined by living sent as the message of God's love.

Success was surrendering to a beyond-self mission for living that put the interests of others as more important than self.

We have a wired-inside connective need for one another because we are made in God's image. He is love, according to John (1 John 4). Since God is love, and His love is for each of us, and His desire is for us to live in loving and sincere community with one another, then we will live in abundance when we experience His love through our love for one another. That kind of connectivity must be a definitive characteristic of not only our own lives, but also of each local expression of the church.

[wrap-up]

Speaking of church, in chapter 3, I will make some suggestions about rethinking church. I mention this now, because the way we think of our live and of right and wrong and of success has significant implications upon how we think of church

In light of rethinking right and wrong and rethinking success, and in preparation for the coming chapter, let me suggest a definition of church that is as simple as "people who follow Jesus together." This would be a more apt definition according to the New Testament, as opposed to the building on the corner that we tend to call church today. As individuals, we must rethink our live in the context of how we relate to both our church family and the culture around us. We must also, as people who follow Jesus together, as His church, live for more than our own sense of right and wrong and our own accomplishments. If we would live sent, and therefore live beyond ourselves, then it would actually help us clarify right from wrong and propel us to the kind of success we were created to have.

As His church, we have a responsibility to humanity to be God's letter of love. That's why He started this movement that He called the church almost 2,000 years ago. So that we would love each other as He intended, as His people, as His family. And, so that we would do more than "go to church," but rather be the church to the people we encounter every day, loving them as He loves them.

As we rethink our live, let's surrender our lives to be the letter of His love that God has written us to be. And, we may have to rethink church too.

[CONSIDER and CONVERSE]

[1] What are some practical examples of how we live only for ourselves?

[2] How does 1 John 4:19 lay a foundation for us to understand how to rethink our live?

[3] In light of the good Samaritan, what is the difference between right or wrong and doing people right or wrong by our choices?

[4] What are some practical ways you can live out a redefinition of success? Write them down and commit to pray about and act on them.

2

rethinking your connection

(knowing the sender)

[a story_Ted]

*T*ed surfs. His neighbor does too. He and his neighbor were going to surf. On the way, they got on the topic of church. His neighbor knew Ted was part of our church family. He had also remembered Ted telling him that our focus was a little bit different. Less on gathering, although that was important. More on sending, which was the real story of the church anyway. This intrigued Ted's neighbor.

They talked a bit more about it and paused to surf. On the way home, Ted's neighbor brought it up again. He mentioned "being the church" instead of "going to church." His neighbor—who had experienced church in the past as a ritualistic religion and had been wounded by a few self-righteous people—began to grasp a different possibility. Maybe Jesus intended the church to be sent, not gone to.

He asked Ted, "So, are we church right now? Here in this truck? Talking about this stuff?"

Ted replied, "Yes." And he continued to live sent to his neighbor. Here is an excerpt from an email Ted sent me the night I finished this chapter:

> "As an update, we went surfing a couple of weeks ago and spent the entire ride back talking about denominations, church culture, and a real relationship with Jesus. He told me that he has made a commitment to Christ. It was a special time."

Now that's what living sent is all about.

Once, I fried a portable DVD player. I'm not proud of it. Actually felt dumb.

We were heading over to a Florida beach for some vacation. We had packed the portable DVD player to show the kids movies on rainy afternoons and to watch movies together at night as a couple. One problem. I forgot the power cord. You know, the cord that makes the DVD player come alive.

I stopped at the local Walmart to see if they had a universal cord. They did. More than I wanted to pay, but I bought it anyway.

We got back to the room. I unpacked the cord and plugged it in. I failed to read the instructions, though. A universal power cord like that has about six different voltage settings. I had no idea that it had different settings until after I plugged it in. Common sense might have told me to check that, but I was still reeling from the price I had just paid. I didn't think about it, and I had no idea the DVD player had a specific setting for voltage required. Until it didn't work anymore. It called for 9 volts. I had plugged it in at 12 volts. It wasn't good.

Needless to say, we didn't watch many movies that week. Probably not a bad thing.

It's interesting, but we tend to go through life kind of like that. Looking for stuff to plug into, hoping it will give us the power for life we desire. Looking for the right connection. Problem is, much like the DVD player, we were actually created with a specific life-source in mind. When we plug into other sources we hope will bring life, we tend to malfunction because we weren't made to connect with those sources. We don't work like we were intended to work, or worse, we quit working altogether.

Have you ever stopped to think about our attempts at spiritual connection in that way? What about the way that we approach connecting with God? Even though the Scriptures make it clear that He loves us and graciously and unconditionally invites us into daily relationship with Him, we still struggle with pleasing God, getting life right, and performing well, religiously speaking.

Could it be that, much like self-indulgence, self-righteousness can also cause us to malfunction? Both begin with "self" after all. The indulgence stuff is easy for people in church culture to point out and call bad.

The personal pursuits of righteousness are not as easy to recognize, since we are doing God stuff that we think may please Him.

For example, what have come to be called spiritual disciplines by many people (praying, fasting, reading the Bible) have become more of a burden and a checklist than something healthy in our relationship with God. We probably need to rethink these too.

I actually once heard, in the 1990s, a guy considered an expert on spiritual disciplines speak on the subject. He passionately challenged us to become immersed in the habits of the spiritual disciplines, because, and I promise you, I am not misquoting him here, "We need to practice those daily habits in order to drag ourselves into an experience with God."

Really? Drag ourselves? Like I don't want to connect with the One who made me to connect with Him?

Don't get me wrong. I understand that the havoc from the choice in the Garden of Eden, the pain that death has wreaked upon us, and the shame that comes with it often cause us to approach God very timidly, and even try to avoid Him. For the most part, though, these feelings are mostly due to a warped view of who God is and how He wants to connect with us. We have an incorrect view, if you will, of the Sender, mainly because of the way those who have been sent are acting.

Maybe a friend who claimed to love Jesus betrayed you. Or a father didn't act like the heavenly Father at all. Or a spouse seemed holy but turned out to be holier-than-thou. Whatever it is, I admit there are things that the evil one uses to send us looking for another life-source. But we were made to connect with the Sender, and we don't need habits to drag us into an experience with Him.

We need to connect with the One who made us, who desires to connect with us, and who has written a message of love on our hearts. He is sending us to deliver that message of love to the rest of humanity who have been deceived into thinking untrue thoughts about the Sender. When we deliver that message, not only will they see who the Sender really is, we will see what life is really all about. It is abundant when we give away what has been given to us, because God keeps giving it to us in abundance so we can keep giving it away. Pretty cool.

So, how do we connect with Him? Like an iPhone or a BlackBerry that allows you to stay constantly connected to your emails and other forms of communication, how do we live in constant connection with the Sender? I think it is a crucial question, because all of us are spiritual beings on a human journey longing to connect with something or someone that gives us purpose and meaning beyond ourselves.

Here are three thoughts to consider concerning our connection with the Sender.

[rethinking obedience]

Obedience is evidence of relational connection, not just doing the right thing or following the rules.

Most people I meet, especially if they say they are Christians, really want to "do the right thing." Earlier, we spent a little bit of time thinking about what Jesus taught about right and wrong. The conclusion was that it is based in the foundation of loving God and loving our neighbor. So, how might this cause us to rethink our connection with regard to obedience?

If doing the right thing or being obedient is more than just following the rules, then what is it? I would suggest it is the evidence of relational connection. In other words, obedience happens because we love.

If right and wrong are based in love, this must be the case. This must also be the case, because Jesus said so. In John 14:15 (WE), He said, "If you love me, you will obey me." Obedience will come as a result of this love relationship, this love connection that we have with Jesus as we walk with and listen to and respond to Him daily.

What's so cool about that John 14 statement that Jesus made is the context it was made in. It gives us a clue as to how we can obey, and how obedience happens out of us. It blossoms out of us as we listen to and say yes to the Spirit of Christ leading us in this life.

Earlier in the Gospel of John in chapter 10, Jesus emphasized this in another way. He said:

"Let me set this before you as plainly as I can. If a person climbs over or through the fence of a sheep pen instead of going through the gate, you know he's up to no good—a sheep rustler! The shepherd walks right up to the gate. The gatekeeper opens the gate to him and the sheep recognize his voice. He calls his own sheep by name and leads them out. When he gets them all out, he leads them and they

*follow because they are familiar with his voice. They won't follow
a stranger's voice but will scatter because they aren't
used to the sound of it."*

–John 10:1–5 (*The Message*)

Jesus told this simple story, but they had no idea what He was talking about. I guess He faced that a lot. So, He tried again:

*"I am the Gate for the sheep. All those others are up to no good—
sheep stealers, every one of them. But the sheep didn't listen to
them. I'm the Gate. Anyone who goes through Me will be cared
for—will freely go in and out and find pasture. A thief is only there
to steal and kill and destroy. I came so they can have real and
eternal life, more and better life than they ever dreamed of. I am the
Good Shepherd. The Good Shepherd puts the sheep before Himself,
sacrifices himself if necessary. A hired man is not a real shepherd.
The sheep mean nothing to him...I am the Good Shepherd.
I know my own sheep, and my own sheep know me."*

–John 10:6–14 (*The Message*)

You see, Jesus is calling us to listen to Him, to know His voice, and to respond to Him.

An implication of that passage is that there are a lot of other voices out there. Now, not to make you feel like you are crazy, but admit it. You hear a lot of voices every day, calling for you, vying for your attention, asking for you to give focus here and there, and asking for you to make this choice or that choice.

If we are really committed to being the church and living sent and living on mission like God has called us to, then hearing the voice of the Sender is paramount. We not only have to be able to hear His voice, we also must be able to discern the voices that are around us.

You see, what we need is to develop ears for Him and a heart that hears Him among the many voices. What we need to focus on is living every moment as though we live with Him, room with Him, go to work with Him, abide in Him, and simply belong to Him. We are His.

Now, when we think of being a Christ follower in that way, it changes things. Be honest, a lot of times when we think about being a Christ follower, we think about the next ten things we ought to be or ought to do to be good for God. How that would change if we actually trusted and believed that being a Christ follower is listening to God and doing what He says. It's not finding the right formula for right living and then patting ourselves on the back at the end of the day.

One of the dilemmas in church culture is focusing too much on the doing. We focus too often on what we need to do to become more and more spiritually mature. We want to be strong Christians. We want to feel valid about our spirituality and feel accomplished in our spiritual maturity. In our minds, we think the more we do to develop our personal spirituality, the better we'll be as Christians. It's the common motivation for what people call the spiritual disciplines.

In God's reality, though, these things do not define us. The more we move toward spiritual arrival, the further away we are from God. Being a strong Christian is not a biblical concept. We need God desperately. When we are weak, He is strong. When we listen for His lead, desperate to say yes, He blossoms obedience in us as we respond to Him. Living as though that is true is more akin to being spiritually mature than living as though we are strong and have arrived and need Him no longer.

Listen to what Samuel tells King Saul in the Old Testament of the Bible when Saul began to put on the front of religiously pleasing God, all the while calling on mediums to summon the dead for guidance:

Do you think all God wants are sacrifices—empty rituals just for show? He wants you to listen to him! Plain listening is the thing, not staging a lavish religious production. Not doing what God tells you is far worse than fooling around in the occult. Getting self-important around God is far worse than making deals with your dead ancestors. Because you said No to God's command, He says No to your kingship.

–1 Samuel 15:22–23 (*The Message*)

The New Testament speaks of our identity and our spiritual maturity too. In the Gospels, Jesus teaches that God has made us as spiritual as we will ever be, and He is calling us to listen to and abide in Him (read John chapters 10 and 15).

Church culture has emphasized what we do as what defines us. I would suggest that Jesus taught that whose we are is what defines us. We are His, and we are becoming more and more His every day. The evidence of being His comes when we listen to His lead and follow Him. Our life then is shaped by a love relationship, a constant connection that creates obedience in our lives.

In the same way, as I heard it explained by a teacher, an acorn is as much of an oak tree while it is still an acorn as it will ever be. But we know it is an oak tree as it is nourished to become one. Our obedience has more to do with whose we are and who we are becoming than it does with who we are now and what we have done to this point.

There were a few things that Jesus spoke adamantly against in the Gospels. One of them was religious, self-righteous, checklist living for God. It doesn't mean that the things that people call spiritual disciplines are not important. It just means that our motivation behind doing them can't be to get better for God or to feel like we are doing good for God. The motivation especially shouldn't be to drag ourselves into an experience with God. It has to be so that we can know Him better, hear Him better, and respond to His voice.

We need to rethink obedience. I want to suggest to you that living for God, being His church, is more about listening and responding to Him than it is about just doing the right thing for Him. Sometimes in church culture, we get caught up in that, and we say, "Well, I do a lot for God," when in essence we miss that tight relationship that He desires with us.

So, how do we listen to Him?

[rethinking prayer]

*P*rayer is the breath we need to live sent. Prayer is the constant communication for that relational connection that we need.

Let me first suggest that prayer is no spiritual discipline. It is not something we do to drag ourselves into an experience with God. It is a must. It is like breathing. And, you don't discipline yourself to breathe.

I'm not at all saying that people who take hours out of the day to pray specifically for people or for wisdom are misguided. If the Spirit leads us to pause and pray in that way, then we better. I am simply suggesting that, like Paul taught in 1 Thessalonians 5:17, we must "pray continually."

If prayer is a never-ending communication with God, then certainly it is not just kneeling next to my bed and saying stuff to God 24/7. It is a constant spiritual connection, and one that is spent mostly listening on our part. It is like that iPhone or BlackBerry, where God could at any moment, at any time buzz in, send a text message, and communicate with us. And, we could at any time communicate with Him.

If we would think of prayer in that way, it would transform the way we connect with God. Like our cell phones, we never want to lose them and never want to lose that connection. They have all those numbers we once memorized but don't anymore. If we lost them, we couldn't call anyone. We need that. We want that around.

Even better said, we need it more than our cell phones. We need to pray as though it is the breath for life.

We must stop seeing our lives as so busy and so important that we need to interrupt it to pray. Maybe, instead, we should see everything else that keeps us so busy as an interruption of the conversation between us and God. How would that change daily living for you?

My friend Mike told me about someone in his family wearing her Bluetooth earpiece constantly. All the time. So much so, that even when he speaks to her, he doesn't really know if there are three people in the conversation or just two. So, there are times when Mike is talking to her and she will all of a sudden say something to the person on the other end of the connection.

That's prayer. Every time we are in a meeting, every time we are on a date, every time we are with our friends, every time we are with our neighbors, every time we are driving alone in our car, we are not alone. There is another Person with whom we are in a never-ending conversation. What if we lived like that? In every conversation, God was always on the line and could speak to us or we could speak to Him at a moment's notice. He is. We need to be ever listening to Him too. Why? Here are some reasons.

[1] So we can respond to and live out what He prompts us to do. Kind of like a teleprompter. We are living daily life, and His Spirit says, "Do this." And we do it. If we were never listening to Him, if the Bluetooth wasn't on, if we weren't always in that conversation with Him, we might miss something that He was telling us to do.

[2] Because we also need to know when He is saying, "Stop and talk to Me." It is a conversation with God, so we do speak to Him, correct? When I look at Jesus' life, you know what is really amazing to me about prayer? He periodically stopped to be alone with His Father. It isn't that He just woke up every morning at 4:30 and did it. In fact, the Scriptures teach that He did it sometimes in the morning, sometimes in the afternoon, and even late at night. Instead of a checklist event for Him, it was a relational dynamic. It was His Father saying to Him, "Hey, stop, and talk to Me."

Not only that, but Paul wrote in Romans 8 that when we stop and talk to God, the Spirit can actually tell us what to pray. Just in case we don't know or are so troubled or are speechless.

So, not only do we hear Him say, "Stop to talk," His Spirit tells us how and what to pray. How amazing is that?

[3] We also need to be listening and aware so that our hearing stays unclogged. Have you ever noticed when you begin to ignore someone's instructions how much easier it is the next time to not listen? That's what happens when we begin to live like we don't need to listen to God. It gets easier to ignore His voice. Before long, according to Hebrews 3, we can find ourselves deaf to His voice. That is a scary thought.

In fact, Hebrews 3 goes as far as to call ignoring God's voice sin. Sin very simply is when we say no to God. You don't need a more complicated definition than that. When God asks you to do something, and you say no, you start turning a deaf ear to God. Hebrews 3 warns that you may turn a deaf ear for so long that you can't hear Him any more. Maybe God doesn't want us to sin because it isn't about breaking rules. Maybe He doesn't want us to sin because He doesn't want there to be relational disconnection between us. Maybe He doesn't want us to sin because it can cause us to go deaf towards Him, and He wants us to get rid of everything that clogs our ability to listen to Him.

So, how can we know when He is speaking to us? How can we discern His voice in the midst of the many voices crying for our attention?

[rethinking the Bible]

The purpose of the Bible is not to be some road map for how to live. This is obvious if for no other reason than it is abridged. It doesn't contain points on every facet of living. It's more than that.

It is a story that has purposefully been preserved to acquaint us with the God who wants to become closer to us every day. It is a filter for the many other connectors that are attempting to seduce us to connect with them. It is the story of how God has communicated with and interacted with and pursued man with His love. And when we read it, we are better able to recognize His voice in our everyday lives because we learn about how He spoke and how His voice was leading others in the Scriptures.

If prayer is like breathing, connecting us with the Life-Source so we can live sent, then reading the Bible is like nourishment, giving us the energy to respond to the Life-Source in our daily living. Better said, it is like nurturing a love relationship, reading a living Word, as God calls it, in order to know Him and be able to recognize His voice as we listen to Him. Prayer and reading the Bible go hand in hand. Coupled together, they are key enablers for following the Sender and living sent.

Furthermore, what we learn from reading the Bible becomes a filter of sorts for the daily grind of life.

Kind of like a coffee filter. Like the daily grind, the coffee beans are ground up. And like the daily grind, we don't want to consume all that's been ground up. Instead, we place the grinds in the filter. The hot water of life comes through and what comes out on the other side is what we take in.

Like weak coffee, maybe that illustration is weak, but hopefully it communicates the point. What we learn from reading the Bible allows us to filter out the many elements of the daily grind that we don't need so that we can take in what we do need. We can discern God's voice among the many in the daily grind and respond accordingly.

Maybe God preserved His Word for us to read, so that we can become more and more familiar with Him and get to know Him well enough to think, "Wait, I hear that voice, and that's not like God. That's not like the Living God that I read about, and I'm getting to know His heart and His life. I'm getting to know what He thinks. I'm getting to know what I should be about, and that doesn't match up."

Or, we might say, "Yes, that's God. I've read something like that. I'm getting to know His voice. I need to say yes." His Spirit prompts us in our hearts and minds to respond to Him in that way.

[connected to live sent]

So, could the purpose of prayer and reading the Bible, simply stated, be to hear His voice and filter out the other ones we don't need to listen to? Are we reading the Bible to know God and to listen to His voice in that way? Are we listening to Him not only for our personal gain but also for our personal mission as His letter of love? Obedience comes as I grow in that interactive, love relationship with Him, as I live sent.

How freeing is that? Freeing enough to motivate us to live sent and tell the world of the God who loves us all and desires to know us all closely in that way. Instead of thinking of our connection to God in terms of how we must be responsible and do the right thing, may we rethink our connection in terms of being "response-able." Able to respond to Him because we are getting to know Him and His voice and responding to Him as He leads us.

Let's remember how much God desires for us to listen to Him. How much He desires for us to be in constant connection with Him. How much He desires to give us life and for us to live life without malfunction. How much He loves us with an amazing love.

[CONSIDER and CONVERSE]

[1] What are some ways that you connect with God? Do these feel like a burden, or are they a natural joy in your life?

[2] Read John 14:15 and commit it to memory. Why is this verse so essential to rethinking obedience?

[3] What is the significance of 1 Thessalonians 5 (specifically verses 16–18, which urges us to "pray continually") to rethinking prayer?

[4] What were some of the reasons suggested for why we should pray?

[5] If someone asked you, "How do you hear God?" what would you tell them? Are you experiencing constant connection with Him, understanding that it is necessary to be steadfast to listen even when He seems silent?

3

rethinking church

(gathering to send)

"*J*'ve tried every religious flavor you can try. And there's something different here. It's just right. I've never understood Jesus this way before," said Malcolm.

He is a middle-aged man who said he had seen it all, pretty much. He'd tried all the options. Sought different angles on truth. Tested the waters in various spiritual expressions. But what he saw among the people of our church family—the genuine love they had for one another, the kindness from his neighbor, the way the men weren't afraid to hug and express love, how laid back people were and confident in this God who loves us. He experienced it over the course of several months and was hooked.

God's letter had never read this way before for him. This near. This loving. This real. Malcolm said he began to read the Bible, more to know God and be able to recognize His voice better every day rather than out of some religious obligation. He shared it with his son, who also began to read the Bible and encourage his dad and ask questions.

Malcolm is a gourmet cook. Several ladies I know covet certain recipes of his. He began to see that as a way to live sent to people around him. When they were sick or had needs, he would cook them a meal (the Guinness beef pot pie is out of this world). He saw friendship as something to be given, whereas before it was something to be avoided in fear of disappointment.

He is trusting again. All because he read God's letters.

[gathering to send]

Is it a fair statement to say that for some time now, people in general have defined church as a place you go to on Sunday morning to worship? Whether we think that is the definition of church, it certainly is a fair description of how we tend to talk about and act about church. I would suggest that there is so much that we need to rethink regarding that definition, especially in how we talk about it and live it out.

The principle exists that you reap what you sow. I hear people teach "love your neighbor" and "go into the world locally and globally and be a missionary every day." I see signs that promote a way of living to reach people for Christ. I know of groups that push people toward discipleship and growth. But what do all these really mean in context?

I ask that question, because there is a very important principle in group leadership dynamic (and in parenting, friendship, coaching, and a whole lot more) that is often missed here. It is this: it's not what you teach, it's what you emphasize. Being a missionary, loving your neighbor, and getting involved in discipling are all great things to teach and push people toward. But they are more importantly great things to emphasize over and over again in more than just words. Something is not being emphasized when it is just talked about. It is emphasized when its message influences both what is said as well as what is done. Something is emphasized when the practical, day-to-day strategic purpose of a specific group reflects that emphasis in everything its members do.

[the church is a "who"]

*L*et me give you an example. I have personally never met a "preacher" who disagrees with me on this statement: The church is not a place or an event. She is a who. The church is people.

I have heard preachers teach that very statement on more than one occasion within their specific context. However, the bridge from philosophy to practice can be a long one. What I mean is that, they teach it, but then they turn right around and communicate these messages in some form (signage, Web sites, handouts, etc.):

- Such-and-Such Church . . . a place where you belong.
- Invite a friend to church!!!
- See you at church Wednesday night!
- Who's missing from CH _ _ CH? U R!

- GOAL—900 in Sunday School. 1,200 in church.
- Church Campaign Fund: $70,000,000 (and this is for more buildings on a central campus)

In addition, the tendency is to put something on the church calendar for people to be a part of every night of the week. Now in some cases, there is not an expectation that you be there for everything. But in other cases, there is this unwritten expectation that you are there for everything, and if you are not, people think you might not really be committed.

Like I said, the bridge from philosophy (thinking a certain way about something) and practice can be a long one. Let's come back to the original question and unpack it.

Is it a fair statement to say that for some time now, people in general have defined church as a place you go to on Sunday morning to worship?

First, is church a place or an event? Did you know that the New Testament of the Bible refers to church in some form more than 140 times? I can't find one single occasion where the reference is to a place or an event. While it is certainly true that it often is referring to people who gathered together, it is still referring to people. The early church gathered in many ways, with one another and within their community, and did life together daily, not just weekly. So, church is not a place.

Next, church also isn't some event we go to on Sunday morning. The early church gathered in many ways together. In Acts chapter 2, the early church is described as praying together, breaking bread together, listening to the apostles' teachings together, fellowshipping together, and sharing all they had with anyone who had need. They deeply loved each other, all week, and deeply loved their families and neighbors and people in the marketplace all week. They didn't go to church. They were the church. And we, too, are to be the church every day.

Furthermore, the suggested statement of how church has been defined implies that we go to church on Sundays to worship, as if that is the only time during the week that we worship. Now, you may not think this is a big deal, but people often miss the multiple opportunities during their daily lives to worship because worship has been emphasized (though not necessarily taught that way) as singing together on Sunday morning.

Throughout the Bible, both Old and New Testaments, you see people worship in multiple ways, encountering God and responding to Him through song, through prayer, through connection with people, through difficulty, through victory, through tragedy, through shame, and much more. And all of these were not at a gathering on Sunday morning. They happened in ordinary, everyday life.

Could it be that people have emphasized the church as a place so much that gathering at a central campus at a specific weekly time has become the main way we think of it? Could this way of thinking actually hinder us from being the church and living with the daily purpose Jesus intended His church to have? It seems we let ourselves off the hook when it comes to doing life deeply with one another, because we did church this week already on Sunday.

[more than semantics]

This is more than just a language issue, more than semantics. It is evidence of the need to rethink so that we can renew how we are being the church. I know, I know. You know the church is people. You even hear preachers and priests teach that from time to time. Great! People need to hear that. But, is it being emphasized?

This is not only important for those who already follow Jesus or those who might be connected to a church family doing life together. It is also important for those who don't yet follow Jesus but are searching for real and abundant life. Like the woman at the well in John 4. Jesus, tired from traveling, was resting at a well in Samaria when she came to draw water. He asked her for a drink, and she expressed some shock that He, a Jew, would even speak to her, a Samaritan, since the two groups were divided on several points, including religious practices. Furthermore, Jesus did not condemn her as her townspeople had. To them, she was a bit of a "loose woman," having had many husbands—and living with a man to whom she was not married at the time. Jesus did not condemn her behavior. Instead, He connected with her at her core beliefs.

Jesus met her in her way of thinking about worship and church (even though she would not have called it church). She asked him about place—Jerusalem or Gerazim. Jesus told her that place was not the point.

Worshipping connected through the Spirit and in the fullness of truth—what God intended her to be—was what mattered. She had stumbled around location and division among the Jewish religious emphases and the Samaritan religious emphases for some time. That, along with some personal shame, hindered her from truly encountering God.

So God came to her. Jesus met her where she was. He challenged her idea of the proper place and how she thought of worship, and He transformed her into a worshipper.

God wants more than for us to just show up to worship. He wants us to be His worshipper every day. Then, when we show up to worship together with the church at a worship gathering, our worship together at that one time in that one place with that group of people will become a reflection of and a celebration of what we've been experiencing with God all week.

Do you know of anyone looking for another good event to go to or another time slot to fill in their schedule? I don't. But, I meet people who are looking for abundant life and who yearn for a cause that makes their lives significant. They are searching for something much bigger than themselves, not just another item to schedule that they feel obligated to attend.

So, if all we ever do is speak of church as this thing we go to or this place down the road or this building with a steeple, how will our culture ever understand that following Jesus is a viable spiritual option every day? The best spiritual option? What they were made for, even? That's a big deal.

It is important to think of and talk of church as a who instead of a what because Jesus did. And, if we really do, it will affect not only our language, it will begin to affect how we are being the church daily.

[two examples]

Here's an example that quite possibly backs up my little hypothesis. In my seminary days, I had a very cool professor who always challenged the norm and spoke of "simple church" before it became as popular as it is today. He asked me a question one day when we were hanging out. The question: What one person had the most significant impact on Christianity in the twentieth century?

I thought for a few moments. Several names passed through my mind.

Billy Graham seemed too obvious. But, with a disclaimer, I answered with Billy Graham. My disclaimer was that I was sure there was someone more significant who was not as obvious a figure as Graham, or he wouldn't be asking me the question. My professor's response might surprise you.

He said he thought the most impactful person on Christianity at the dawn of the twentieth century was Mao Zedong (1893–1976), the foremost Chinese Communist leader of the twentieth century and principal founder of the People's Republic of China. He expounded.

When Mao Zedong came to power, it had not been long since Christianity had been introduced by missionaries to the people of China. The number of Chinese who were following Jesus at the time was relatively minimal. When the twentieth century came to a close, the number of Christ followers in China was estimated at 80 million. Probably more, though, because of so many underground that we can't count.

In contrast, when Communism overtook Russia in 1917, the church had already been established. Cathedrals of brick and mortar were abundant. People equated Sunday and buildings with church. Under Communism, the church did not flourish there like it did in China. Why? Because the construct was church as a what. When the what got oppressed and controlled by Communist leaders, it became stagnant.

In China, however, it flourished as a who. People did not quit "going to church" because they had no concept of "going to church." They just kept on being the church.

Here's a modern-day example. Hurricane Katrina ravaged the town I grew up in. New Orleans is an earthy city, full of artisans and ethnic groups and chefs and everyday folk who make up an eclectic cultural melting pot known as the Big Easy. If you really want to get a feel for it, search "Chuck Perkins New Orleans Poet" on Google. He is a poet from New Orleans who has written a poem that describes my hometown better than any other description I've seen. Well, that earthy city became a muddy waterhole when Katrina's storm surge and rain overpowered the levees that held the canal waters running several feet above the city. Chaos and death and confusion ensued, and an event occurred that those involved and those whose hearts are tied to this expressive city will never, ever forget.

Many churches that existed before the tragedy did not continue afterward. But, some did. When I talked with local friends and pastors about this dilemma, there was a common denominator that became clear. Those local church families that were being the church—not just going to church—before the storm, continued to be the church after the storm. The churches defined by their buildings and events were swept away in the flood—both figuratively and literally—because their structures were demolished.

My home church family lost their building. The whole thing. But their ministry lives on and their heart continues to beat for the people of the city they love. The Big Easy was not so easy during that time. Still isn't. But the people who were being the church before the storm are still being the church afterward. That's a fact.

[church 168]

It seems to me that the church has been taught as a who by most teachers I know in North American and European church culture. However, what has been emphasized is definitely more of a what, a place, or an event. What has been sown is "come and see and a master teacher will feed you." What has been reaped is followers of pastors and/or other good teachers who have:

- made Sunday mornings a sacred cow;
- equated discipling with getting more people to the place where they can hear the pastor;
- developed spiritual nourishment patterns defined by gluttony on the Sunday worship experience, as well as on the words of the pastor on Sunday mornings, all the while starving themselves;
- become lazy when it comes to living out the teachings of Jesus the rest of the week.

Surely pastors have not intended for this to happen. While it may stroke the ego of these equippers, it has stifled the daily ministry of everyone else. And it is the daily ministry of everyone else that seems to be much more important according to the New Testament, and much more influential according to the stories of the people of our culture.

Why? Could it be that the daily ministry of the church as a whole tells a story and engages people in a way that pastors never could on Sundays? Could it be that the credibility of daily living is and always has been a much more significant form of influence than what one individual tries to communicate?

Not that what pastors communicate is unimportant. Not that the role they play as equippers is not necessary. But Sunday mornings cannot be viewed as just "fueling stations" any longer. They must be viewed as "post offices," gathering and sorting mail in order to send out those letters into daily culture.

Process that for a moment. How much more focused and intentional would you be in each of your relationships if you thought of each encounter as the very mission we are called to as the church? How would you rethink church if you understood that you are a letter containing the message of Christ's love, and that you were intended to live out and carry that love to the world?

My friend Johan is a local pastor whose church family partners with ours from time to time. The phrase he uses to emphasize this is "Church 168." There are 168 hours in the week, and we need to be "being the church" all 168 hours!

With a post office, letters are always going out. This is a much better way of thinking about Sunday morning. How would what happens on Sunday morning change if we thought of it this way? What happens on Sunday mornings—is it a catalyst for sending out letters or just an attraction, attempting to draw more and more people in?

If church is nothing more than a Sunday morning refueling station for you, think about this. Aren't you going to run out of gas during the week? Don't you need more nourishment than that? That way of thinking—Sunday morning church as a fueling station—is such a self-absorbed, consumeristic mind-set. It is like eating a bagel on Sunday morning, even if it is with that yummy, flavored cream cheese, and expecting that one meal to satisfy you for the whole week. That's ridiculous. About as ridiculous as putting the burden of your spiritual nourishment on one person who is supposed to flavor messages each week so they're good enough to sustain you until you can come back the next Sunday.

What if we have been thinking of gathering on Sundays and how we fuel up there as the most important element of church, when all the while it has caused us to forget how we should be the church daily? Has that way of thinking, that emphasis, hindered us from living sent beyond the four walls where we gather? What if we gathered as the church less and lived sent as the church more? What if we worried less about the church as an entity to preserve and more about being the church as people?

Another friend, a guy who connected with our local church family through a couple that was simply being the church to them, wrote me a letter when he and his family moved away. He had done life with us for a while, and his takeaway was significant. Here's an excerpt:

When we first connected with Westpoint, it was to provide our son with some solid moral principals that would help shape him as he grew up ... or so we thought that was the reason. In reality, God was the one doing the molding and

the shaping. With my wife and I having grown up in church, we both were wonderful at talking the talk of being Christians and were both failing miserably when it came to walking the walk that accompanied it. God used our son to bring us to our knees and surrender ourselves to Him.

We felt loved from the very beginning. It just got better from there. Our eyes were opened to an entirely new path of how a church should function. Love Jesus ... love people. ..love people the way Jesus loves people. What a concept! Westpoint is not about being a church with this huge list of religious do's and don'ts. It is about living with joy, living with stress, living with pain, living with your neighbors and coworkers ... just living life. Letting Jesus live through you every day of your life. Not judging people, not condemning them, but loving them. Walking with them through both good times and bad. Doing this thing called life together.

Church was always such a chore for me before we were with Westpoint. Now church is me. I am the church all day every day.

I have been blessed with Westpoint to have so many people to call upon if I need help, guidance, a shoulder to lean on, or someone to help me when I stumble (and we all stumble). Someone to hold me accountable in my words and actions. Our family is taking a part of each of you with us to Texas. We are taking the concept of love we have learned from Westpoint and will plant that seed in our new location. We will water it, nurture it, and let God run with it as only He can

Being the church every day. Church 168. Living sent daily as a letter from God to a people He loves and wants us to love too.

Very seriously, we must rethink church. We cannot emphasize the central campus and what happens inside the four walls on Sunday mornings any longer.

Church culture in general has become more "come and see" than "go and be." The letters (people sent by Christ) are, for the most part, sitting in the draft box of the email inbox or on the post office shelf. It's like we have a message to deliver, but we are expecting people to come to our house and get the email or stop by the post office and pick up the letter. Think of it this way: I have an email inbox for more than just gathering emails. It certainly does that. But it actually exists to communicate fully—from and to. It isn't worth much if I don't send emails back, if I don't respond. What I fear has happened in church culture is that we have emphasized writing emails but never sending them. Like when I write an email draft and save it for review. What if I never sent it? It would just be "saved" sitting in the draft box. Saved but not sent. Sounds eerily like much of church culture today.

We must go beyond just gathering. We must gather to send.

[go this week and be the church]

We close our Sunday morning gatherings the same way each week, simply as a point of spoken emphasis. After we've done all we're going to do and are about to release everyone to live sent during the week, one of us will say something like this:

Like we say every week. You don't go to church. You are the church. So, go this week and be the church.

May we all do that, and be that letter every day. May we see the vitality of gathering as a response of worship together, celebrating what God has done in and through us throughout the week. May we then leave that gathering, connected to the One sending us, so that we will continue living as this movement He started long ago called church.

[CONSIDER and CONVERSE]

[1] Read Acts 2:42–47. How would you describe the daily life of the early church? How can you and the followers of Jesus you do life with begin to live out each element in this text?

[2] Compare and contrast the two examples of the impact of communism on the church. What is the major difference between the church in China and Russia? What lessons can we learn from these two examples?

[3] This week, take an inventory of how you speak of and refer to church. When the week is over, see if you speak of church as a who or a what. Do you think this is significant?

4

a fueling station or a post office?

(why is the local church important?)

*B*ob leads a Sunday morning small group for his church family. He admits that the focus of this small group has not always been about living sent. He gave me this example to illustrate.

One Sunday morning, Bob's pastor challenged those in their large-group gathering to try a small group for at least six weeks. The challenge was given with a guarantee of sorts—that the people who tried it would quickly find out why doing life with other people so closely was worth it.

Mary took up the challenge. She showed up at Bob's small group, which meets at an elementary school, that very morning following the large-group gathering. Group members gathered around tables in clusters of five or six. She came in about ten minutes after the group began. The room was pretty full. As a result, she did not join a table but instead sat in a chair near the group but not necessarily within it.

At the conclusion of the group time, Bob talked about the need to do life together more intentionally. He asked for any final comments that needed to be shared. Mary, in a share-the-truth-in-love moment, courageously let the group know she was glad they wanted to do life together at higher levels, but they were missing the obvious.

"You say you want to do life together, but you let me sit outside the group for the entire group time. I don't know if that means you don't like me or I look funny. You don't know me, but less than a year ago, I lost my 21-year-old daughter Grace to a four-year battle with cancer. Today, your pastor gave a challenge in the worship service. He said that anyone who connected with a life group for six weeks would experience life-changing relationships. Well, this is week one," she said.

It was an awkward and amazing moment. Bob thanked Mary for her courage and honesty, then challenged the class to pray through the implications of her comments. As Bob closed the class in prayer, the living sent transformation began. While he prayed, the women in the group gathered around Mary to hug her and pray for her. When Bob closed his prayer, they continued. As the men reset the classroom furniture for school the next day, the women in the group concluded their prayer. Through the hugs and tears, a transformation did take place.

Mary brought her husband, David, back to the Sunday morning group. Instead of David and Mary having to look for a table cluster to join, people were looking for ways to live sent to David and Mary. In that six weeks, and beyond, the life group walked with them through the first anniversary of Grace's death, an ambulance ride to the hospital with their son, Mary and David's work with a recent youth missions experience to Honduras, and a variety of other experiences that happen when you care enough to live sent together.

On another occasion, around the same time frame, Bob's group discovered that Nick, one the group's newest men, had a serious form of liver cancer. The group had already come together to live sent to Nick in a number of ways. There were commitments to pray, to visit him in the hospital, and to help financially while he was out of work. In one effort to live sent to him they planned a night of bowling together.

Bowling may not seem like a heroic effort at living sent, but the experience allowed the busy professional men in the group to love on, laugh at, and laugh with Nick in a time that was not funny at all. The men left the bowling alley that night with that awkward-last-night-of-camp feeling. God had sent them as a letter to help Nick laugh. The moment still has a lingering effect on the men in the group.

Nick's journey is not over, but the effect on Nick has been profound as shown in this email thread that follows:

From Nick:

Dear Bob and Tina,

As I finally start to feel better I would like to take a moment and thank all those incredible people whom through praying, writing, and just supporting have made this journey I have been on, one where God truly was and is present. I am so grateful for all my friends there, and we are fortunate to have one another.

Love and gratitude to you all!!

From Bob:

Nick,

Good to hear from you! Believe it or not you have supported us in your journey. We learned what radical faith looks like in a family facing unbelievably challenging circumstances. I know your journey has not been without questions, disappointments, and setbacks but don't question your faith because of that. Following a God we have never seen into places we have never been on the belief that He is actively involved in our circumstances is not natural; it is supernatural! Your life is an offering to God and a blessing to us.

We love you guys.

That's the effect truly living sent can have on both the individual and a group that commits together to be a letter.

[the purpose and importance of the local church]

I wanted to dig a bit more into the concept of the church as a fueling station versus as a post office. So, here are some thoughts about the purpose and importance of the local church.

First, why do you think church is important? I would suggest to you that your view of the church's purpose affects your view of the importance of the church. Let me ask it this way. Do you view the church as a fueling station or a post office?

If you view church as a fueling station—a place that you go to get fueled up spiritually—then consider two questions. One, if you are connected with a local church, are you connected for reasons that are self-centered or missions-centered? And two, how would you define spiritual maturity? Let's consider those questions one at a time.

If your common thought when you leave a Sunday gathering of believers involves whether or not you got something out of that experience, then you may be self-centered in your reasoning for connecting with a local church. If you spend more energy concerned about the music and mood than you do about the intent and the emphasis, then you may be self-centered in your reasoning for connecting with a local church.

If this is the case, then you, for the most part, are a consumer of church. A self-serving approach to the purpose of church is epidemic in America. Until leaders quit trying to appease the consumer, then consumers will continue their addictions to personal worship experiences and leaders will continue to burn out under the pressure to create that same attractive, compelling environment every week. As has already been declared, we cannot expect to make the bride of Christ (the church) any prettier than the Cross already did. And yet week in and week out, are we doing anything more than feeding the craving of the masses addicted to hip music and an undersold gospel? Thus, church is a fueling station that requires the "cars" to keep coming back for more while leaders become exhausted.

Why not see the reason for connecting with a local church more like a post office? Letters don't just gather together to sit. They gather together to be sent. In fact, they are not focused on just gathering for the sake of gathering for a moving event. They instead are gathered around a mission, united to live sent together. Letters arrive at a post office not to stay there, and you especially become disgusted if a letter gets returned there. Letters gather at a post office to be sent. The reason for connecting with a church family is not because you enjoy the band or the preacher. The reason for connecting is because you believe in and want to unite around others' compulsion to give love away and the mission for which they live.

a fueling station or a post office?

The church of America has for too long defined spiritual maturity in terms of knowledge and speculation rather than in terms of selflessness and participation. We know so much and have become gifted at speculating about what doctrines are sound and what methods are good. But would the poor of our cities describe us as generous? Would the wounded among our acquaintances describe us as inviting? Would the lost of our communities describe us as marketers of self or servants of others? I don't think we are as spiritually mature as we think. I am not.

American preacher, author, and speaker Francis Chan once offered an amazing illustration. He was describing what Jesus really intended for His followers, and he declared that a few people had approached him and told him what he was suggesting is too radical and not realistic in American culture. They told him there was more of a middle road between the two extremes of being lost and being fanatical for Jesus. Chan went on to give an illustration about how this middle-road group tends to think they are spiritually mature but in fact may be fooling themselves. Consider this.

Chan said it would be like saying to his daughter, "Please go clean your room." But when she returned, she declared one of two things to him. Either that she had memorized what he asked of her and could happily recite it to him. Or that she had gathered her friends together and spent two hours studying and discussing what he might have actually meant when he asked her to clean her room.

It sounds silly, but is it a description of a typical American Christian? Is it a description of me? The church is good at reciting verses and enrolling in small-group studies and even debating doctrinal issues. But Jesus didn't highlight any of these when He spoke of the evaluation of our life in the end. Instead, in Matthew 25:34–40 (NASB), He said:

"Then the King will say to those on His right, 'Come, you who are blessed of My Father, inherit the kingdom prepared for you from the foundation of the world. For I was hungry, and you gave Me something to eat; I was thirsty, and you gave Me something to drink; I was a stranger, and you invited Me in; naked, and you clothed Me; I was sick, and you visited Me; I was in prison, and you came

to Me.' Then the righteous will answer Him, 'Lord, when did we see You hungry, and feed You, or thirsty, and give You something to drink? And when did we see You a stranger, and invite You in, or naked, and clothe You? When did we see You sick, or in prison, and come to You?' The King will answer and say to them, 'Truly I say to you, to the extent that you did it to one of these brothers of Mine, even the least of them, you did it to Me.'"

Now I am not suggesting that memorizing Scripture or studying the Bible or small groups are bad. Not in any way. I am only suggesting that if the extent of the evidence of Jesus in my life is limited to biblical knowledge and small group involvement, then I am not necessarily spiritually mature. We have thrown around phrases like "strong Christian" for too long, creating environments where personal achievement is highlighted more than the needs of the community around us. Spiritual maturity, according to John, isn't about how I can linger on in Christian rhetoric, but rather about how I live my life giving Jesus' love.

Here's the point. Our understanding of spiritual maturity affects how we live as the church. A significant hindrance to living sent is a misunderstanding of the pursuit of spiritual maturity. It's not self-improvement or self-actualization. It's not self-anything. When the goal of our spirituality is self-anything, it usually results in self-righteousness. Self-assurance and personal fulfillment are not our end game. Denial of self must be the first step every day (Luke 9:23). When spiritual maturity is defined in terms of beyond-self rather than in terms of myself, then my understanding of the importance of the church will line up more with the intent Jesus had for His church. A post office more than a fueling station.

[so, why is the local church so important?]

Simple. Because we cannot live sent effectively and enduringly without each other.

Jesus commanded us to love one another in John 13:34–35. This love for one another is the mark of Jesus' disciples. He said so in verse 35. Therefore, we must live and move on mission alongside other followers of

a fueling station or a post office?

Jesus who are living sent. The size and method is irrelevant. But we need each other to effectively live sent.

Jesus also prayed for His followers to know oneness with the Father the way He did while on earth, and He prayed for His followers to live out that oneness with the Father through their oneness with each other. In fact, He prayed all of this in John 17:18–23, and therein specifically states that the world will believe in the One who was sent through the oneness of those living sent now. And this is the work of God, John 6:29 tells us, for the world to believe in the One who was sent. So Jesus prayed for us to live sent together so that through our togetherness around this sentness the work of God would be done.

Jesus also promised on many occasions that living sent would not be easy. A cursory read of the New Testament proves this, simply by the persecution that His followers endured. And the book of Hebrews is completely devoted to calling the church to live sent together with endurance. Gaining encouragement from each other to stay on mission was essential. Read Hebrews 10:23–25 (NASB):

Let us hold fast the confession of our hope without wavering, for He who promised is faithful; and let us consider how to stimulate one another to love and good deeds, not forsaking our own assembling together, as is the habit of some, but encouraging one another; and all the more as you see the day drawing near.

If you have ever worked on a bulk mail marketing project, then you understand the marketing principle behind the importance of bulk mail. Less than 1 percent of the people who receive mass marketed bulk mail respond to it. That's why companies send out so much at one time. Multiple touches. Many messages read. And the many together create the response hoped for.

Well, the same is true for the local church. Jesus commanded it. Prayed for it. And the New Testament highlights it. The local church matters because when many believers are living sent together (multiple touches) and many people are seeing the nearness of God's love (many messages read), then more and more may come to believe that God so loved the world (a response to His letter). This is the only explanation I can come up with for what Jesus meant by what He said in John 14:12.

The person who trusts me will not only do what I'm doing but even greater things, because I, on my way to the Father, am giving you the same work to do that I've been doing. You can count on it.

Hopefully more than 1 percent of those loved will respond to His love, but no single success is a small one in God's eyes. Regardless of the outcome, over which we have no control whatsoever, we must live sent together. Greater things beyond simply gathering await!

[CONSIDER and CONVERSE]

[1] Why do you think the local church is important?

[2] How would you differentiate between the church as fueling station and the church as post office. Are elements of both OK?

[3] Someone where you work comes to you and asks, "How would you know if someone is spiritually mature?" What would you say?

[4] Why is our togetherness vital to living sent?

5

a letter, not a personal to-do list

(Jesus' intent for the church? self-serving
consumerism or beyond-self mission?)

[a story_Joe]

*J*oe is from Scotland. My friend Bill introduced me to him. Bill is from Scotland too. That's only significant here because Joe now lives in Peru. Here's the story as I know it.

Bill's mom had a heart for the children of Peru. Before she died, she helped fund a mission there to mentor and feed families and children in a Peruvian village. There is an issue there that unfortunately is not unique to Peru. Once many boys reach a certain age, their impoverished families cannot afford to feed them. So, they cast them out in the streets. Some are killed while living on the street. Others try to fend for themselves. Others are sold into various forms of human trafficking. All of them are way too valuable and beautiful to have any of this happen to them.

Joe went to Peru with a volunteer group and helped build a school. He was hooked. Back in Scotland, he was an electrician, and a fairly successful one at that. But, pulled by the calling to do something about what he had seen in Peru, he sold everything he had to move there and live sent among the impoverished families. Now, he gives his life away trying to help boys and girls, as well as feed hungry families.

He also met his wife there. A Scot and a Peruvian living sent together. There can, from time to time, be some perks to living sent.

[what is the gospel?]

*T*he gospel of Jesus in and of itself is a letter of sorts. It is good news. It is sobering news too. A letter from God through a Living Word. Not to oversimplify it, but I would suggest that the Living Word (Jesus) declared three very to-the-core, life-changing, mission-sending messages.

First, God loves us unconditionally. The fact that God loves us unconditionally leads to the second declaration of the gospel, which is that even while we were still sinners and even before we said we were sorry, Jesus graciously and lovingly died to restore us and fix what we had broken. The third declaration is the sending declaration.

Now, with the first two declarations in mind, we must live sent to share the message from the Sender. We must continue to know and love the God who unconditionally loved us first, and we must stand firm only because of what His grace did with our sin. Inscribed with this message of love and grace and embodying what these first two declarations of the gospel have done to us personally, we now live as God's letters of love, putting skin on this gospel within our very relationships and even as we go around the world.

The point—the purpose—of this gospel given to us is that it would be given through us. When we believe this good news, it does not suddenly shift from being a letter to being a personal to-do list. It does not go from being a letter from the generous and gracious Sender to now being a message to be hoarded greedily and gainfully by the recipient of the news.

[self-serving consumerism]

Stay with me here. I am focusing on this for a chapter because I am afraid that the church of America has, without meaning to, made the gospel into nothing more than a self-improvement mechanism rather than a denial-of-self sending movement. It's as if we receive the letter of love then try to make ourselves good for God. But the gospel itself says we cannot make ourselves good, thus it must not be the gospel's purpose to put us into a position as "saved" people to now make ourselves good enough. That would be completely contradictory to the message of the good news itself.

Paul referred to the gospel as "the *power* of God for the salvation" (Romans 1:16). The word *power* in the original language is the root word for our English word *dynamite*. It blows stuff up. Based upon the teachings of Jesus and the rest of the New Testament, I would suggest that what it was sent to blow up was my selfishness and my self-absorbed pursuits. Jesus wrecked people's way of thinking. How I live for God became how I live

a letter, not a personal to-do list

with God and what I gain from religion became what I give. A letter passed along, not turned into a personal to-do list.

What if the gospel was intended not only to be a letter to us but to become a letter through us? What if the gospel becomes most evident among us when we are made to become (by the transforming power of our gracious and loving God) a selfless people rather than a self-serving people? Didn't Jesus die for so much more than our opportunity to enroll in self-improvement classes, to engage in personal worship experiences, and to sign up for an occasional service project? Wasn't the church intended to exist for more than self?

Paul wrote about this intention for the church on many occasions. In fact, I would argue that it is the central theme of Paul's writings. He was sent to be a letter to the Gentiles, but throughout his ministry he carried a burden to be a letter to the Jews, declaring to them that they had become self-serving and had missed the intended mission of God through them (Romans 9–11).

First Corinthians communicates this message. In chapters 12 through 14, Paul challenged the very divided, self-preserving, self-promoting believers among the church of Corinth. He wrote to them that they were to move beyond focusing on being known individually for their gifts to being known collectively for their love. They were to be letters, if you will, of the gospel alive among them, rather than checking off their personal to-do lists of who was the most important or who impacted the church family the most with his or her spiritual gift.

When I read 1 Corinthians 13, I often ask this question—what is the real purpose of this beautiful description of the ways love is expressed in our lives? Why did Paul throw this selfless diatribe into the middle of a very pointed chastisement of some very selfish behavior?

Here are four thoughts to consider regarding the purpose of 1 Corinthians 13:

[1] It was not for Paul to give a few how-tos for personal self-improvement.

[2] It was not intended to be a pity-stick that the church of Corinth could beat themselves with because they weren't doing right.

[3]   Paul was probably offering a contrast between the actual characteristics of relationships in the church of Corinth at that time (divisiveness, impatience, unkindness, jealousy, dishonesty, immorality) and what the relationships should have demonstrated (patience, kindness, humility, forgiveness).

[4]   Paul was probably giving a description of what it would look like if the gospel of love and grace was present in them, offering a picture of God alive among them and in their relationships.

God alive in us. His love tasted instead of the bitter flavors of our self-absorbed lives. The Head of the church (Jesus) must be noticed more than any of us who try to act like the head of the church. This is important because when we alone are noticed, then the living and loving God is too often disguised by our desire to be seen and the letter of the gospel is concealed by our self-promotion.

[beyond-self mission]

So the church is a letter of the gospel to the world around us. Followers of Jesus are supposed to bring out the flavors of God's love and highlight the colors of His grace in our everyday relationships. Remember what Jesus taught in Matthew 5:13–16? Let's read it from *The Message*:

> "Let me tell you why you are here. You're here to be salt-seasoning that brings out the God-flavors of this earth. If you lose your saltiness, how will people taste godliness? You've lost your usefulness and will end up in the garbage. Here's another way to put it: You're here to be light, bringing out the God-colors in the world. God is not a secret to be kept. We're going public with this, as public as a city on a hill. If I make you light-bearers, you don't think I'm going to hide you under a bucket, do you? I'm putting you on a light stand. Now that I've put you there on a hilltop, on a light stand—shine! Keep open house; be generous with your lives. By opening up

a letter, not a personal to-do list

71

John picked up on this "being generous with your lives" thought and also communicated that the intent was to be a beyond-self letter rather than a personal to-do list. Not only did he record the new command Jesus gave to His followers regarding selflessness (John 13:34–35), but he also wrote that "God is love" (1 John 4:16). There in 1 John 4, John wrote that if we are "in Him" then He will be "in us" and "through us." His love controls us. Compels us. Moves us.

Paul picked up on the same thought, expressing it on multiple occasions. But specifically, in 2 Corinthians 5:12–21, where he laid out the gospel of Jesus and its implications in a progression of verses, in which I would suggest lies the clearest expression of what the gospel would look like now alive among us. Check it out (from *The Message*):

We're not saying this to make ourselves look good to you. We just thought it would make you feel good, proud even, that we're on your side and not just nice to your face as so many people are. If I acted crazy, I did it for God; if I acted overly serious, I did it for you. Christ's love has moved me to such extremes. His love has the first and last word in everything we do.

Our firm decision is to work from this focused center: One man died for everyone. That puts everyone in the same boat. He included everyone in his death so that everyone could also be included in his life, a resurrection life, a far better life than people ever lived on their own.

Because of this decision we don't evaluate people by what they have or how they look. We looked at the Messiah that way once and got it all wrong, as you know. We certainly don't look at him that way anymore. Now we look inside, and what we see is that anyone united with the Messiah gets a fresh start, is created new. The old life is gone; a new life burgeons! Look at it! All this comes from the God who settled the relationship between us and him, and then called us to settle our relationships with each other. God put the world square with himself through the Messiah, giving the world a fresh start by offering forgiveness of sins. God has given us the task of telling everyone what he is doing. We're Christ's representatives. God uses us to persuade men and women to drop their differences and enter into God's work of making things right between them. We're speaking for Christ himself now. Become friends with God, he's already a friend with you.

How? you say. In Christ. God put the wrong on him who never did anything wrong, so we could be put right with God.

We are moved to live sent as a letter from God by the love of Jesus. His love, given completely because of who He is, not because of how lovable we were, made everything right between us and God. And now, that kind of compelling love, mysterious love, change-everything love transforms our very relationships, allowing us to see each person through the lens of the love that we have "in us" rather than the feelings of impatience, frustration, woundedness, or bitterness that we might have toward them.

His love changes us. His gospel letter transforms us for good. The evidence of that fact is seen when His love changes everything else in and around us.

The point: Love is central to God, and thus must be central to His followers and His mission to which He has called them. Paul is writing in 1 Corinthians 13 a very simple, focused message: You say you love God and have been changed by Him. If so, then He will be tasted and seen in you in place of the tastes and sights of selfishness and personal advancement.

A letter instead of a to-do list. Beyond-self mission instead of self-absorbed consumerism. Not, what will the church do for me? Rather, how will I go and be the church for others?

How beautiful the gospel looks lived out and declared rather than just being highlighted and channeled for personal improvement. Following Jesus is about more than personal gain. Living sent is about more than personal to-do lists.

[CONSIDER and CONVERSE]

[1] Someone asks you, "What is the gospel?" What will you say?

[2] How are selfish flavors being tasted in your life, rather than the flavors of Christ's love and grace?

[3] Based on an examination of 2 Corinthians 5, is the gospel alive in your life and among your relationships? Why or why not?

[4] Do you spend more time focused on personal development than you do on being generous with your life? Does this need to change? How?

6

you are not junk mail

(love like you are loved)

[a story_Rob]

*R*ob and his wife and son live in uptown New Orleans. They are letters into an artistic, diverse, beautiful section of an artistic, diverse, beautiful melting pot of a city. Rob is being the church, planting the love of Jesus, and watching a new expression of a local church blossom called Vintage. The people who call Vintage their church family are living letters alongside Rob into the lives of lots of people who are spiritually minded, but disappointed by broken relationships and false claims of fulfillment.

Rob and the Vintage family are out in the community daily in their respective spheres of living. They live, following Jesus and giving His love away, as friends to the people in those various spheres. When questions arise about spiritual things, conversations ensue. Groups of people who are naturally doing life together form. Then, with the intent to love like Jesus loved, those folks from the Vintage family walk closely with those groups. Sometimes there's a pool party. Sometimes there's a service project. Sometimes they study the Bible. Sometimes they watch a game. All the time, though, the letter of God's love and hope come near is being read in the lives of those who follow Jesus. At all times.

Mark is a great example. He coaches men's tennis at a local university. He is simply doing whatever it takes to genuinely love the tennis players who play for him. He has a ready-made small group of guys among whom he is making disciples as Jesus asked His followers to do in the Gospel of Matthew. Mark hangs with the guys. Teaches them tennis and about life. Is there to listen to them. Is there when they have need and when they celebrate. From time to time, he cracks open a Bible with them. But every day, the living Word of Jesus is alive in Mark and His message of love that has been written on Mark's heart is read by those players.

Rob and Mark and the Vintage family are living sent.

I hate junk mail. It does nothing but fill up my recycling box or go in the trash. It is worthless to me. I can't stand it. Do I need to tell you how I really feel?

Sadly, I meet lots of people who actually feel about themselves the way I feel about junk mail. In the email metaphor, they would consider themselves sitting in the junk email box, not to be received again. This is very sad to me. Although, it's no wonder people feel this way. When the selfishness of our world writes itself into our lives through degradation shame and win-at-all-cost competition and lack of long-term, loyal commitment and so much more, it's no wonder people feel like junk—hopeless and purposeless. We have all been the brunt of someone else's self-absorbed choice. Not to mention, Jesus said the evil one is out to steal life from us any way he can (John 10:10).

We truly all do want to be loved, as the songs say, and we truly all want just a little R-E-S-P-E-C-T. In fact, based on what was first declared by God to be "not good," I would suggest that feeling alone is the base fear for all of us. We don't want to be alone. We want to know we are loved.

This must be another component of the havoc wreaked in the Garden. Before the fruit of the tree of All Knowing was eaten, Adam and Eve walked in the fullness of the One John said "is love." They must have known they were loved. And still they ate of the fruit, thinking they knew better, and later wishing they did not know as much as they came to know when they ate of that all-knowing fruit.

What in the world am I saying? That even though we have wired in us an awareness of a God who made us and loves us, we learn to not love and not trust and not respect because of the ways we have treated each other since the Garden.

You've probably heard the saying, "I know I am somebody, cause God don't make no junk." I am sure grammar enthusiasts have loved that one. But if you look past the double negative, you find a foundational principal for living sent. We can love because we are loved. We can be a letter to others, carrying a message that they are not junk, because we trust that we are not junk either.

you are not junk mail

[a bundle of "not junk"]

recently thought of this when another bundle of not junk arrived on the scene. In 2008, my wife and I were blessed with our fourth child. She came right before Christmas. It prompted many thoughts in me, including thoughts about why God put on human skin, became a baby.

With each new child that I am blessed to hold, I am made more and more aware as to why. I feel like God's Spirit informs me with just another glimpse into the why of that first Christmas from His perspective. And He does it every time He gifts us with a new baby. So, why did He become one?

Because a baby is given. Because a baby makes things new again. Because a baby brings life. Because a baby exudes joy. Because a baby smells like heaven. Because a baby implies hope. Because holding a new baby is so peaceful. Because a baby needs us.

Could it be that God needs us? The mere sound of the question hints at heresy of sorts. The divine needs the divisive? But He does. He must. Why would He go to the trouble of giving His love to us like He did? Maybe because at His core, He is love, and love must be given. And so He made us to give that love, which makes us seemingly necessary as the ones He gives it to. And so He became a baby.

And in spite of knowing that God Himself crafted us for His holy purposes, the evil one can still convince us that we are junk. This doesn't make sense, because God has clearly demonstrated His love for us. We are worth dying for. He loved us enough to prove it.

In Jesus' day when He walked the earth, rabbis would say stuff like, "You have heard it said, but I say to you . . ." However, it wasn't common for one to come along and give a new command.

Jesus did. In John 13:34–35, He told His followers, "A new command I give you: Love one another. As I have loved you, so you must love one another. By this all men will know that you are my disciples, if you love one another."

Jesus affirms His love for us, and then, calls us to love like we are loved. To love like we aren't junk. To love others like they aren't junk either. It begs a question. How would I describe how Jesus loves? I need to ask this question, because He commanded me to love like He loved. And I pray for wisdom for each of us to know that answer as we know Him more and

Live Sent

more daily. Here are some thoughts I would suggest.

He loves us. Period. My dad says that's the "redneck" definition of unconditional love. He says he has the authority as a redneck to declare the definition as such. And he's right. About the definition, I mean. Jesus loves us unconditionally. No ifs, ands, or buts about it. No matter what we've done. No more today than yesterday. No less today than tomorrow. He loves us. Period.

He chooses to love us. His love is not based on how He feels at the moment. His love is not just a warm-fuzzy kind of love. He certainly wasn't feeling a warm-fuzzy on the cross. No "Boy, this makes Me feel good loving you like this." No "Man, you guys are so lovable, I think I will take three nails for you." He chooses to love us regardless of how lovable we are or are not.

He loves us so that we will love. He wants to see us become all that we were meant to become. And, He knows that we experience the fullness of life we were made to experience when we know His love fully and freely give it away. He knows we find true life when we give love. And, so He loves us so that we will be able to give love as generously as it has been given to us.

Jesus asked us to love as He loved. Based on these three descriptions of how He loves, how will I now love? Let me ask three questions here for you to spend some time processing.

[do you believe He loves you unconditionally?]

I am convinced that the hardest thing for humans to believe and accept is unconditional love. I have seen people take absolute rejection, believe they probably deserved it, and keep on walking. However, I have seen people struggle deeply when someone loves them through a situation when they know they do not deserve that love at all.

This is foundational for someone to follow Jesus, and therefore, fundamental for someone to be able to live sent. We must trust that God loves us like He says He does and like Jesus demonstrated. We must believe. This is the "believe" part of John 3:16. We find life "now and forever" (usually translated "eternal life") when we believe that "God so loved the world."

You cannot give love like Jesus did unless you believe He loves you. Period.

[love—earned or given?]

I asked this of a friend who, as he says, had grown up in church. His response is common, even among those who call themselves Christian. He said that love must be earned. Maybe you think that way. If so, stop and reflect for a moment. Did we earn Jesus' love? Someone once answered that question by saying to me, "That was Jesus. He's different."

Yeah, maybe. But He did ask us, command us, to love like He loves. And we must be able to do so, at least with His help, if He bothered to command it.

Thankfully Jesus doesn't wait around or expect us to earn it. He loves out of who He is or we would have never been loved. And we must love out of who He is in us, or we will never follow through on His command.

Even if you could declare yourself a good person (even Jesus avoided that adjective about Himself—read the Gospels and you'll see it), you have demonstrated selfishness at some point. This means you probably lived in such a way that contradicted the selfless ways of the Sender, the God who made us. So, you have the need for forgiveness, for a Savior, for someone to give you love unconditionally.

Jesus stepped into time and fully communicated, "This is how God loves you. Period. No ifs, ands, or buts. And He showed it in this way—by giving His only Son. Believe that He loves you. Period. That He loves you no matter what. And you will find life, now and forever."

Do you believe? Do you trust that what Jesus did is enough for you to have a connection with God that grows closer daily and that is based in an everlasting love?

You can. Because, as John wrote in 1 John, God is love. He lavished His love upon us. He laid down His life to show us the depth and reach of His love. And He loved us first, so that now we can love.

Do you love for how it makes you feel? Or do you love so that others will feel love and give it away, knowing that you may never get anything in return for your love? This is a more significant question than you or I can understand. I say that, because I believe it is the great distinguisher between the way God loves and the way the world speaks of love.

The Bible says that God is holy. I have heard most of my life that holy means "set apart." The question I have commonly asked, though, is this: How is He set apart? Besides the obvious, that He is God and we are not, I mean. Could it be because He is completely selfless?

I know I would get some argument here from people who are angry at God or who see Him as a self-righteous zealot who controls us with force. But I see nothing of the sort in the Scriptures. Even in the Old Testament of the Bible, the times when God slaughters a large group or even women and children (which I admit I struggle with sometimes as to why that had to happen), even then, God's purpose is to preserve a specific people in a specific land for the sake of a specific Messiah to come at a specific time to carry out a specific mission that would provide restoration for all the world. The only thing that is not specific to this event is its impact—it is not time-specific. In other words, the Cross may have happened at a certain point in time, but its impact spans all of time. All of this so that all the world might be restored unto the God who is selfless enough to put on skin, come to us as a Son of God, and die for us that we may all be restored as His sons and daughters.

He is completely selfless. I have often wondered why God gets to be jealous but we don't. The Scriptures declare that He is a jealous God, and yet we are told that jealousy on our part is a sin. What's up with that?

It must come back to the fact that sin is rooted in selfishness rather than in whether we keep a list of rules. Selfishness versus selflessness. It must be because God is actually selfless in His jealousy, whereas we are selfish in ours. He loves us so much He can't bear our rejection of the love we were made to have in abundance. And so, selflessly, He hurts and pursues us.

Jesus told His followers in John 15 about His "set apart" kind of love and His command for them to love as He loves and how in love you give up the rights of position and personal fulfillment. See what you think:

you are not junk mail

81

*"This is my commandment: Love each other in the same way
I have loved you. There is no greater love than to lay down one's
life for one's friends. You are my friends if you do what I command.
I no longer call you slaves, because a master doesn't confide in his
slaves. Now you are my friends, since I have told you
everything the Father told me."*

—John 15:12–15 (NLT)

At this point in John's account, the Passover before Jesus' crucifixion had already happened. They had eaten the last supper. He had already washed the disciples' feet. Talk about giving up owner status. Talk about being set apart as selfless. That was for the lowest of the lowest of servants to perform. When you read John 13, John even wrote that Jesus had been given all authority. Then, a verse later, John wrote that Jesus took off His robe and washed the disciples' feet. It's like John was saying, "Jesus was the most powerful man in the room. Most powerful man in the world, even. And, He set that aside along with His robe and washed their feet."

Jesus concluded this servant of servant's act by telling the disciples, "You also do as I did to you." You go and love like this. You go and lay aside position and feeling and anything having to do with self. That's being holy.

Looking like you have it all together and that you always do the right thing—that's being holier-than-thou.

[live and love like you are not junk]

Man. There is such great risk in loving like this, isn't there? We so often tend to love just when it's safe, just when we know there's a return, just when we know we'll at least see something good come of it for us. Why?

Could it be because of how that makes us feel? Could it be because of this selfish need we have to know the score of our performance? Could it be because we live thinking we are selfless, when maybe we are really living with a selfless selfishness?

I heard Danny Wuerffel speak about this subject. He talked about how, when he was the national championship–winning quarterback for the University of Florida, people loved him. It was easy to serve then because people always loved back. They always appreciated it.

When he joined the New Orleans Saints, however, he was just another guy on the team and just another apartment renter in the city. He said: "It was a whole lot easier to serve when it was appreciated. It was a whole lot harder to serve when I was treated like a servant."

It's not safe to love like this, like Jesus did, because we might get treated like junk in the process. We might get disrespected or devalued. But we must give love nonetheless. Jesus did. He was spat upon. Beaten. Disregarded. Mocked. And still He loved.

Come back to this question: Why did Jesus love like this? What did He hope would come of it? I think the answer is found throughout His teachings, but here are two specifically:

"If your first concern is to look after yourself, you'll never find yourself. But if you forget about yourself and look to me, you'll find both yourself and me."

—Matthew 10:39 (*The Message*)

"The thief comes only to steal and kill and destroy; I came that they may have life, and have it abundantly."

—John 10:10 (NASB)

When you commit to love someone—marriage, friendship, child, whatever—are you committing to love them for what they become and what they get out of it, or for how you feel and what you get in return?

I understand. I do. I, too, know how hard it is to love like this. But we can. We must be able to, because He commanded us to.

I grew up in New Orleans, in the inner city there. Great place. Great church family there that loved and served families in the heart of the city. Outside groups would come into town for what they called missions trips to New Orleans. We always appreciated it. Really, we always did.

My friends and I could always tell a difference between the groups that came to town with an air of superiority and the ones who came to town to give love selflessly. The ones we would say were stuck up would come acting like we needed to be fixed and they could fix us. They would treat us like junk that needed repair. And if we responded well, they would be happy. But if we didn't, they would seem disappointed, like the trip was a waste.

On the other hand, the groups that seemed to give love selflessly never seemed disappointed in the outcome. They didn't seem to care about the outcome. They seemed to care about us more than the performance result of their trip. They seemed to want to know us, to call us friends. To simply be a friend. Like they knew we might connect with the true Friend that they walked with. Like they knew if they simply loved, we might connect more deeply with the One who loved us and would give us life. They loved us because they wanted us to know life, not because of what it did for their life.

The richness of giving love like that—as Jesus said in Matthew 10—is that we find fullness in life when we do. Even if we aren't looking for what we get out of it, we still somehow do. It's that lose-to-gain economy that Jesus operates in.

So, remember that you are not junk mail. You are actually a letter containing the message of love from the ultimate Lover, intended to live sent to a world who desperately needs to know they aren't junk mail either.

[CONSIDER and CONVERSE]

[1] In regard to being a follower of Christ, why is it important for you to "love like you are loved"?

[2] What are your responses to the three questions posed about the love of Jesus?

- Do you actually believe that He loves you unconditionally?

- Do you think that love, respect, and trust must be earned, or must they be given?

- Do you love people for how it makes you feel, or do you love others as a catalyst that causes them to love, even if you never get anything in return for your love?

[3] Read the story found in Matthew 25:31–46. What is the difference between the two groups, and how does this inspire you to live sent?

7

when mail gets blocked

(a hindrance to living sent)

*M*ark would never call himself an expert in social networking through technological means, so I will. I don't talk to anyone who thinks more naturally about living sent online, through various avenues on the Web, than Mark. He is a strategist who helps church leaders be more effective in starting new local expressions of the church. He is an early adapter too.

Before the public was even talking about podcasting, Mark was talking to me about it. Before the public was really considering the power of Google and YouTube and Facebook and Twitter, Mark was giddy painting the significance for me over a cup of coffee. Before anyone else ever mentioned MeetUp.com to me, Mark was leading a MeetUp.com group of business leaders searching for better understanding about search engine optimization for their respective companies' Web sites.

You might be wondering—isn't Mark a strategist for starting new churches? What on earth is he doing leading a small group of people in business stuff who all showed up at a coffeehouse because they met online at MeetUp.com? Good question. Two answers:

[1] Mark is a Google AdWords Certified Partner. So he knows a lot about the stuff those business leaders are looking for.

[2] Mark loves those business leaders, understands the value that God has declared about him, and wants to communicate to those business leaders that they are worth dying for to God too. So, he has been befriending them, being there for them, answering more than just search engine optimization questions. He is being a living letter of God's love and hope to them. And they are reading the message, while seeing the genuineness with which Mark follows Jesus and loves like He loves.

Mark is living sent in other ways online too. And you can too. Are you intentionally being God's letter through your interactions on the Web?

[a hindrance to living sent]

I don't know what it is, but there are certain Wi-Fi spots where I can't send and receive emails. I check the connection. Make sure I have opened my Internet browser when it's required. Make sure I am signed in for those spots where it's required. But still I get messages like "the mail server has failed" or "email message can't be sent" or "you are not connected to the Internet."

Sometimes that even happens to God's letters to us, doesn't it? At least it feels like it. Often we do it to ourselves. The mail gets blocked. Why is that? Based on what we've looked at so far, it must not be about performance. Maybe it's about relationship. Maybe it's about relational connection and security. Maybe it's about staying connected to the Sender in such a way that the letter goes through.

In this chapter, I want to suggest that the most common reason connections are dropped, and that followers of Jesus are hindered from living sent, is because we believe that we are below-standard equipment.

Let me say right off the bat that I am not at all suggesting that you are "below-standard equipment." Yet, we tend to feel like below-standard equipment. Then, the mail gets blocked and we are hindered from living sent.

People simply do not feel like they are worth enough to live sent, to be a letter from God into culture. That is a lie from the evil one.

God thinks you are worth dying for. Not only that, but He trusts you with the responsibility of sharing His love with the world and being a significant part of His restoring humanity. The living God believed in us enough to come and give us what we needed in Himself, to come and dwell in us through His Holy Spirit, and to call us into a mission daily that has eternal significance and makes everything we do meaningful and purposeful.

Jesus' last words make this calling on our lives to be His letters very clear:

when mail gets blocked

Jesus, undeterred, went right ahead and gave His charge:
"God authorized and commanded me to commission you:
Go out and train everyone you meet, far and near, in this way of
life, marking them by baptism in the threefold name: Father, Son,
and Holy Spirit. Then instruct them in the practice of all I have
commanded you. I'll be with you as you do this, day after
day after day, right up to the end of the age."

—Matthew 28:18–20 (*The Message*)

That's our mission as letters from Him. To carry His teachings through word and deed into all the world—both around the corner and around the globe. What a mission! If our mission is to be the church daily, making disciples as we go, then what do I really need to focus on in order to accomplish that mission?

It would be easy here to insert a formula. However, while the answer is not as simple as a formula, it is certainly not all that complex. It is centered in my very being. Who I am. Who God wired me to be. Why I exist.

[trusting your God-given value]

The essential foundation for living sent, for living the mission God intends for me, is this: I must trust my God-given value.

This essential element is also the essential hang-up. You see, Jesus declared our value at the Cross. He clearly stated there, "You are worth dying for." Understand, this is a declared value, not an appraised value. Remember, He did not go the Cross because we were lovable. He went to the Cross because He loves us, and it is His love for us that makes us lovable. It is His pursuing love that makes us valuable. It is His invitation to be involved in His activity that makes our daily lives worth anything.

I have to be frank with you here. Why would anyone ever want to come on a journey with Christ, if they look at our lives and don't see that we clearly think of it as the most incredible mission ever given? Why would anyone ever be intrigued by the way we live our lives if we don't live in such a way that shows we think God called us off the bench into the national championship game of life? We must treat it as though He's given us the most important mission ever given. It means something. It is not just a segment of our lives—this church thing—it is our lives. To be His letter of love to our family, our neighbor, into the marketplace, into the local and global community, and even on the Web. In every sphere of life.

In order to live like that is the case, we must trust our God-given value.

I mentioned earlier that our value has been declared, not appraised. Did that make sense? Here's what I mean.

Our home, when we signed the contract to build it, was worth a certain price. Well, ten months later, when we moved in, the appraised value had risen nearly $75,000. Ten months later! We moved in and we still live there. In the nearly five years we have lived there, we have seen the appraised value go from below $200,000 to above $400,000 to below $200,000 again. That's in nearly five years. That is crazy!

Well, no wonder our mail gets blocked and we are hindered in living sent. No wonder, because that's how we tend to think of the value of our own lives. We tend to treat our worth as though it is appraised from day to day. Think of the insecurity and turmoil that causes. Think of how it hinders us from the mission we were intended to be living out.

Our value is not like the value of our home—at least not to God. He is not looking at the height of our baseboards or whether we have crown molding or whether we have the right paint or a great kitchen or redesigned bathrooms or wood floors or anything. God is not looking at our outside appearance—what we wear, what we own, what we accomplish, whether we look like we have it all together.

He's not fooled by all that stuff and isn't looking for it anyway. It's like the old realtor trick when they tell you to bake cookies when you are showing your house, so that it smells homey. God sniffs right through that to what really matters to Him.

And what really matters to Him? Check out what God told Samuel the prophet when he was going to find the next king of Israel:

> *"The Lord doesn't see things the way you see them. People judge by outward appearance, but the Lord looks at the heart."*

—1 Samuel 16:7 (NLT)

And guess what! God gives you and me a renewed heart because of what Jesus did. That disconnected-from-the-Life-Source heart that was a consequence of what happened in the Garden, He restores through what happened at the Cross. Therefore, you and I are declared worth dying for. The Living God thinks we are worth dying for, regardless of how we think of ourselves. And, since He made us, we probably ought to adopt His perspective of us and live in that view.

[when we don't trust our God-given value]

If this is the case, if we are worth dying for to God, why do so many of us live like we aren't worth anything? Why do we live like we have no value? Why do we think of ourselves as worthless and meaningless?

I am convinced that the primary intentions of the evil one are to turn us inward and hinder us from our intended purpose. The evil one is trying to convince us to be selfish. It is evident in the self-absorption of humanity and the resulting symptom that the church calls sin. As already has been written, all of us struggle with selfishness. It goes back to choosing our mission. Me or God? If the thief comes to steal and kill and destroy, like Jesus said in John 10, then clearly the intent of the evil one is to get us off track from our intended mission. To hinder us from living sent.

The primary way this happens is when we begin to believe the lie that we are below-standard equipment, rather than believing what has been declared in both word and action—that we are worth dying for.

One of the most defeating traps of selfishness that Jesus' followers fall into is the feeling that they still need to prove their value. It is so amazing that individuals will place faith in Jesus Christ, trusting His gracious death and resurrection as enough for salvation, and then, turn right around and live like their worth still has to be proven.

Why do we live like we think our own value trumps what God declared? Instead of trusting what He said, we are so prone to act like we aren't valuable. When we fall into this trap, we try to get out of the hole on our own. We tend to do one of two things:

[1] We attempt to prove our value through spiritual self-actualization. We try to do the self-help approach and focus on doing things right.

> We become so busy doing things we think are good and that will make us better for God, that we actually miss the mission of giving away what we've been given. Our spirituality becomes a self-centered, religious feel-good that we pretend validates our identity.

Jesus validated us at the Cross. But we doubt that, and go on trying to prove our value. The problem is, while we are trying to prove our value, we are secretly struggling with feelings of doubt that stifle us and keep us self-focused on proving our value instead of living as letters of God's love into culture.

Multiple factors contribute to these feelings. And, passive, defeated living ensues. Whatever has caused us to feel this way, the underlying issue is one of trust. Relational trust, at that. Specifically, trust that what Jesus declared about our value on the Cross actually trumps any circumstance or betrayal or failure in our past, along with any sense of accomplishment we could have, now or in the future. What God feels about us actually supersedes any feeling we have about ourselves. Until this trust is given and its implications are evident in daily living, people who struggle with this go on living stifled and weary, unintentionally living a self-centered life and failing to bring their value into the various relationships God has given them.

> [2] We attempt to focus our energy on stopping what we do that's wrong. We think if we can fix the wrong stuff, we will get it right and then be valuable. Problem is, all this does is focus our attention on what we are doing wrong rather than on the One who did it right. The struggle again is trust, but this time it is more about not trusting unless perfect performance is present.

People who struggle with this think they have not done enough to earn this declared value, so they work harder at getting it right. Do you know anybody like that, who dedicates all their energy trying to correct wrong behavior until they become perfect? It's similar to the self-actualization thing, except with self-actualization, we actually think we are good enough to help ourselves.

when mail gets blocked

A few years back, the New Orleans Saints receivers were, at one point during the season, leading the league in passes dropped, a category in which you really don't want to lead. The local newspaper reporter asked the receivers coach in an interview what they were going to do to remedy this. Three times in the interview, the coach made this statement: "We are simply focusing on catching the ball."

Did you hear that? In the simplicity of that statement, the coach proclaimed a foundational truth found throughout Jesus' teachings: Don't focus on the wrong behavior in order to arrive at right behavior.

Instead, we must focus on the One who is making us right and who Himself did it right. When I trust His performance was good enough to remedy my poor performance, and believe in what He is performing in me over the long haul, then my performance begins to become what He wants it to become, as He works out of me what He has worked in me. Make sense? Because we will never get something right by focusing on how we get it wrong. But we can be changed to blossom obedience when we focus on the One who loves us and whose love in us changes us.

[trust that what Jesus did is enough.]

In both of these attempts to deal with how we feel about our value, the real underlying issue is trust. Do we trust the value that Jesus declared about us or not? When we don't, do we realize what we are really saying to God?

"God, I hear You. I hear You saying we are worth dying for. I hear You say I'm worth something. I hear You declaring value over me, but I don't think I'm worth much. So, your declaration is meaningless."

Now, very few of us would ever say that to God, right? Who would ever look God in the face and say, "Oh no, I know better. I know better." But that's what we do, maybe without meaning to. We don't trust His declaration of our value, so we live stifled and self-centered and weary and hindered from living sent. Like we have below-standard equipment.

A question arises in all of this. What is salvation anyway? I mean, is it just a one-time event highlighted by a prayer and walking down an aisle? Is it just about getting saved from hell? Is it just about an experience? Or, is it about a journey? Is it about trusting what Jesus did was enough for me to "be saved"? Is it also about continuing to trust that what He is and will be doing in and through me is especially significant and very much enough for me to not keep checking my personal spiritual yardstick and constantly being disappointed? Is it further about what He will do—bring me home one day and save me for good? This is how the New Testament teaches salvation.

But maybe we have spoken about salvation in terms of heaven and hell and sin and right living for so long, that we struggle to believe we might be valuable enough to live on a daily mission with and for God. Therefore, we spend all of our Christian energy proving ourselves instead of sensing our declared value and giving away the love that has been so freely given to us.

What if we were actually wired to live sent? What if we were actually intended to give His love away, selflessly living, relating with God and with people, pouring into the lives of everyone we know?

Let's assume for a moment that we were. If we don't trust our value, we won't live as we were intended to live. And things that don't operate like they were intended to operate malfunction. In life, then, person after person, struggling to understand his value and purpose, either never plugs in, or he plugs into other things besides God looking for meaning.

Like the illustration of the DVD player, when an object that has wiring and a power cord never plugs in, the object never operates as intended. Likewise, when an object plugs into something other than what it was created to plug into, it burns out and destroys itself. So maybe our malfunctioning has more to do with the fact that we aren't living according to our intended purpose and less to do with how we are malfunctioning with our bad behavior.

Philosopher and theologian St. Augustine, a church pioneer of sorts who lived just a few hundred years after Jesus, said, "You formed us for yourself, and our hearts are restless till they find rest in you."

What if Jesus came to die on the Cross to remind us of our original wiring and reconnect us with our power source? What if He died not for us to have better behavior, but for us to be able to rest from the weary search of where to plug in and thus live according to our intended purpose? We have forsaken our very wiring for the attractive gizmos around us.

Paul emphasized this in Romans. In the first chapter, he told his Jewish readers that the truth about who God is and how they were to connect with

Him had been written in their hearts—it was within. In Romans 2, he told his Jewish readers that the Gentiles understand the Law and the requirement to love God and people better than they do, because it had been written on their hearts and they were responding to it. In Romans 3, he clarified the desperate need for God, regardless of religious accomplishments and how God intended His people to need Him from the beginning. In Romans 4, Paul emphasized what Jesus did for us was enough to set us right. We can't set ourselves right and were never intended to. In Romans 5, he challenged his readers to embrace this one-of-a-kind of love found in Jesus, who declared our value by dying for us even though we had betrayed Him. In Romans 6, Paul described the freedom we have in Christ and the free gift of life He gave us by fulfilling the Law for us. In Romans 7, he spoke to our malfunctioning when we choose not to listen to God's voice in us. And, in Romans 8, he highlighted the fact that we are not condemned and that we are God's children made to walk in victory and value with Him.

You see, according to Romans, if we choose self over God, we malfunction and miss the gracious gift of life found through faith in who Jesus is. Instead of rules to keep or break, we have a God who loves us deeply and pursued us all the way beyond death to give that love to us. Why would we not want a relationship with a God like that, who very obviously wired us to live in love near to Him?

Donald Miller said it well in his book *Searching for God Knows What:* "It is a very different thing to break a rule than it is to cheat on a Lover." If this is true, then morality is not as much about rules as it is about being true to the way we are wired. In essence, we are denying the very truth within us, the very way we are wired, the very Lover who has made us to live in love and on mission with Him.

This leads to an important question about our purpose: What if righteousness has more to do with purpose than behavior? I have heard righteousness defined as "the completed purposes of God." If that's the case, then God completes His purpose in us when we trust that His completed purpose on the Cross is enough. Then, we get to live in and live out loud that completed purpose in our daily lives. When we set ourselves apart to live according to our intended purpose and listen to God for His leading as we do, our behavior becomes nothing more than a by-product of our purposeful living.

If that's the case, then what's the purpose of the Law? Jesus told the Pharisees that He did not come to negate the Law, but to fulfill it (Matthew 5:17–20). So, it must be important.

Here's the deal in my opinion. The Law leads to death, because as a standard it reveals our selfishness. Our selfishness results in sinfulness and causes us to live malfunctioning—not as we were meant to live. We get what's coming to us when we live selfishly. The wage for selfish living is death and destruction (Romans 6:23) because we lose the very thing we are seeking as we live life only for ourselves and in so doing, we destroy ourselves (Luke 9:24).

So, Jesus died and restores us to what we were meant to be—His worshippers, living daily for a set apart purpose. The Law that the Pharisees thought would lead to holiness and righteousness really led them to a self-righteous and a self-absorbed way of living—whitewashing themselves on the outside and focusing on self-actualized behavior instead of selfless, purposeful living.

In Galatians, Paul said that the Law is the shadow of Christ, the way we were meant to live cast back through history before the Cross. In other words, we look to Jesus for the way we were meant to live. Not for a set of rules for living. The set of rules was given for our provision and protection. When we live according to what God says, life works. It's not always easy, but it works. You see, His commandments for us are not some theological treatise—stuff he thought would be fun to make us do and not do. They are simply practical. We simply work like the Creator created us to work as His creation when we listen to Him and do what He says.

All this said, Jesus changes our purpose from the inside which affects our behavior on the outside. The Pharisees missed the point. They thought they were to focus on behavior. In doing so, they lived an even more selfish life—focused on being self-made religious experts who lived to preserve their image and not God's.

Jesus calls us to live for a bigger purpose than that—His image and His fame. Holiness and righteousness have more to do with purpose than behavior, and more to do with who we are than what we do. Our actions then become defined by God-centered living rather than self-centered living. The law can't bring about that change. The one who fulfilled it can—the One who called us back to what God intended for us in His original covenant. We were meant to live according to His purpose.

In looking at what salvation and righteousness and my purpose really are, I am able to see that I am not below-standard equipment because He has declared me otherwise.

So, what is my purpose? To give myself away into the lives of others and make disciples of Christ. To be a letter of God's love into culture. To live sent. To do this, I have to understand my purpose, what salvation really is, and what salvation means regarding my daily living. In other words, I have to realize that Jesus died so that I could live and give life away, not just so that I could have spiritual peace and spiritual validity as I live a good and right life.

Since this is the case, I must live to "be the church," giving away the love and the value given to me and declaring that God has come near to everyone I encounter in daily life (primarily with actions, and also with words).

So, what's keeping us from doing that? Ultimately, we don't trust that what Jesus did is enough for us to have salvation, be righteous, and actually have a meaningful purpose in life. We don't trust our God-given value. We are not fully convinced that we are valuable enough to actually be a part of God's redemptive purposes, of God's righteousness as He draws others to Himself.

The most crippling issue hindering us from being the church is our insecurity to think we need more than what Jesus did—like good performance or a pastor to do the ministry for us—to spiritually impact the people in our lives.

[each person valuable]

Aren't we each valuable and able to speak value into the lives of those around us? Don't we each have the Holy Spirit? In order to do that, we have to trust our God-given value. It isn't because we are valuable on our own; it's because we are declared to have value and have been commissioned to live sent as a letter of God's love.

Here's the beautiful thing. When we surrender our efforts to be about what He most wants to be about, when we simply listen to Him in the daily things and do what He says, when we actually trust that we are able to bring value to each relationship we have and speak value into people's lives because of His Spirit in us, then we become better in the areas we most worry about and we live according to our intended purpose.

So, for me, being a better person and husband and dad and so forth cannot happen apart from me denying myself and giving all I have to following closely to Jesus, listening to Him and doing what He says that day, in that moment. We have the Holy Spirit. He speaks to us, shapes us, corrects us, guides us, and so much more. He is the living Word dwelling in us and keeping us on mission and purpose.

I am afraid that in church culture, at least in North American Protestantism, we have created one of the very things Jesus eliminated—a priesthood. Christ followers are not living according to purpose, because, for too long, we feel like all the value that exists within the body of Christ was given to the pastors. Because of what has been emphasized, we feel that all the value given for living on purpose and all the value that enables us to speak value into the lives of others was given to the modern-day priesthood. After all, let's just get them there on Sunday and the preacher can tell them about this stuff.

In Hebrews, it was clearly written that we don't need another priest other than Jesus. We have direct access to God. What I am saying is that, as a pastor, I want to lead a revolt. Not a reformation like Martin Luther and a few of his colleagues did, but a "refunctionation." We don't need a better form of how we have done church. We need a return to the function of how Jesus intended us to be the church, to be His letters, to live sent.

I long for the day when each of us as everyday followers of Jesus, who don't get paid to love God and love our neighbor, but who are commissioned to do that in our various spheres of living without compensation, will be highlighted more than the paid guys. Those who follow Jesus in the every day, whether paid or not, are out in the middle of culture, experiencing the beauty and the richness and the depth of the mission that God has given us. When we live as letters of God's love, we who follow Jesus in the every day will experience the abundant joy that comes from seeing that love change the lives of people who read us.

I guess what I am saying is that the "sermons" that you are living every day among family and friends and neighbors and co-workers and classmates are the real messages that need to be recorded and podcast. Thanks to those who ask for our teachings to be podcast, but I want to hear your lives. Read your letters as you live sent. These are words much more significant to the people hearing them. Yours are actions that speak much louder than the polished lectures that ring within the walls of church buildings across the country on Sunday mornings.

Because you have been declared worth reading, and worth dying for, you can trust your God-given value to live sent every day. I heard Francis Chan once teach, "If you believe in what God says about you, there is no limit to what you can do."

Why? Because you have the Holy Spirit in you. Did you hear that? I wish the depth of that statement struck us the way it did in the first century in the early church.

For a moment, can you lay down familiarity? For a moment, can you sit up straight and think clearly here, and remember that God's spirit dwells in you if you follow Jesus? The Living God dwells in you.

I love how a church family in Los Angeles emphasizes this. They don't require months of specific training for someone before they encourage them to go and tell their story about how they met Christ. Do you know what they do? When someone trusts Christ and begins to follow Him, they tell them, "Now, we encourage you, within 24 hours, to go tell your story about how you met Jesus to someone you know." You know why they can do that? Because that new follower has all he or she needs to do that. The Holy Spirit of the Living God dwells in them.

We have all we need to live this out, and to bring a priceless, life-changing value into the lives of the people we do life with every day.

There's this doctrine church leaders have called "the priesthood of the believers." It emphasizes that the everyday follower can hear from, relate to, and speak of the God we follow. We don't need anyone else to do it for us or to get us to Him.

Ephesians 4 says we are all ministers here. What pastors must do is begin to encourage all those ministers to live sent daily rather than to come on Sunday. May those who pastor us actually equip us. May they pour their energy into getting their church members whatever they need in order to bring a priceless value into the lives of others every day. May they do this instead of pouring all of their energy into 30-minute monologues that most people don't remember. Not that preaching the Word is not important, it just may not be as important coming from one person on Sundays as it is coming from every follower all seven days of the week. And, may pastors get out there living sent right alongside those ministers, walking in friendship with them, and encouraging them. And then, we can all live as the church together, equal at the foot of the Cross, each person valuable. May you pray for and encourage those who equip you to live out the belief known as "the priesthood of the believers."

[live sent unhindered]

We can do this! We can trust our God-given value and live our lives giving God's value away into the lives of others. We can hear God whisper to our minds and heart, telling us that word to say or that compassionate act to do, all the while knowing that we were a part of the righteousness of God as His righteousness was lived out purposefully through us.

Like I said in chapter 2, don't stop praying. Listen. Read the Bible. Learn that filter of the voices better and better. Know. Relate to God. Walk with Jesus daily, His Spirit dwelling in you. Live responding to Him. Live sent as His letter of love.

We cannot live on mission if we are crippled by a wrong view of our value. A courageous life won't be lived without us understanding the value we've been given. Every relationship is devalued when we are not coming into it confidently with all God has declared of us and all of who we are. Let's not shortchange our relationships. Let's live out loud the value we've been given into others and live with the courage that God intended for us.

We must. This is a must, because the mail cannot get blocked. It must not get blocked. We must live like we actually are on a mission. We must trust our value, and listen to God, and speak into the lives of others. I really can't imagine what our community would be like, what our culture would be like, what our families and neighborhoods and our world would be like, if every follower of Jesus quit living to prove their value and to perform better religiously, and instead started living on mission to take the message of God's near love near to the people around us.

when mail gets blocked

I'm not talking about handing out tracts everywhere you happen to go. I'm not talking about pulling out the Bible everywhere you go, and saying, "You need to get saved." I'm talking about loving people where they are with the love of Christ, building a friendship with them, and when God prompts, serving them and speaking into their life. If we would do this, humanity would happen as God created humanity to happen. People would be introduced to Jesus. Disciples would be made. And people would be released to live sent as a letter of God's love into culture.

So, the next time you are grilling out with your neighbor or eating lunch with a friend at school or on a date with your spouse or throwing a ball with your kid, be ever listening to God. Trust your value and have the courage to share that value when you sense God's Spirit prompting you. Speak love and value into the lives of the people God has blessed you to be with daily.

An example of this comes from a lady in our church family who caught on to living sent. She emailed me and my wife with an idea to begin a "book club" with some moms she has connected with at her daughter's school. She wanted some ideas on books and Bible study so she could walk more closely with these moms. In essence, she wanted to share the value given to her with them. She did it! A few weeks later, she wrote us this follow-up note:

Hi!

I just wanted to update you both on the "book club" I've started with the moms at my daughter's school. I decided on The Power of a Positive Mom by Karol Ladd. I went back and forth trying to decide what book would be the best. I was so excited! I bought the book and started to read it last week. There's a web site to go visit: www.PositiveLifePrinciples. com. Once you visit that site, there's a link for Bible Study. I clicked on that, and it has info on how to start a Bible study with a free leader's guide for the book!!!

So, we're up and running! I have at least three moms attending Thursday morning. I'll keep you posted! I feel like I'm in over my head! God is working and is up to something!

—Tammy

You don't have to start a Bible study, necessarily. You do have to live on mission, whatever that means for you, as you listen to the Sender and He prompts you. I am convinced that if Christ followers would trust their declared value, more and more would be doing more than going to church. Instead, they would be being the church, living sent daily.

Remember, it's not about you being adequate enough. Your value has been declared. It's not appraised. It's simply about being attentive enough. Listening to God as He leads you daily to live sent as His letter into culture.

May we listen to God daily as He speaks to us and guides us to give ourselves away into the lives of others. May our living sent fulfill that commission that Jesus gave in His last words on earth, and may we make disciples. Other people who begin to follow Jesus, learn His ways and live His ways, cause others to meet Jesus, find abundant life, and begin to encourage others in the same way.

Here's my prayer:

> Thank You, Jesus, for declaring us worth dying for. Help us to be constant reminders of the value you've declared for every person everywhere. Help us to not be blocked by our own insecurities. And may we live sent as the letter of Your love every day.

[CONSIDER and CONVERSE]

[1] What are two things the author states that are reasons why we don't trust our God-given value?

[2] What do you think about the brief summary of Romans 1–8 found early in the chapter? How does this summary display God's desire to be in relationship with us?

[3] Every person is valuable. Think of at least one way to communicate to a family member, a neighbor, and a co-worker how valuable they are to you.

[4] Every follower of Jesus was intended to live sent. Besides what the author suggests, what other hindrances might there be that keep us from living sent?

[5] Discuss ways each of your unique gifts, when brought together, make you even more valuable to the mission of Christ.

8

mail goes to an address

(get to know the address, aka contextualization)

[a story_Melanie]

*M*elanie has seven kids. Her husband works hard. They, like most couples who have kids, walk through the ups and downs of their marriage, growing along the way with one another, all the while spilling their love out onto the beautiful children they are raising. And they're busy.

Did I mention that Melanie has seven kids? No. She is not crazy. She is a hero who lives sent in one of the most significant ways that anyone can. As a mom.

To all you moms out there, Melanie is much like you. She doesn't claim to do it all right. She doesn't pretend it is easy. She isn't looking to write a book on parenting. She even mutters from time to time about how tired she is. But she remains tireless in her pursuit of being God's letter to her husband and kids.

She says that loving her kids, teaching them about loving Jesus, and loving other people are her primary goals as a mom. She says that when she and her husband heard the message of being the church instead of just going to church, they felt a freedom they had not felt before. In their scramble to attend all the church activities, caring for one another had been pushed aside. Living sent not only made their everyday activities eternally significant, it validated the most important mission she and her husband had. The mission of living sent to their own family.

And they do. And they're growing to learn more and more what that means. That God's love letter is read by their kids every time supper is served, every time their legs ache from playing on the floor with the kids, every time her husband romances her with a rose and a refreshing break, and every time she makes love to her husband even at the end of a never-ending day.

To all you moms out there—what you do is unsung, but it's not unseen by the Unseen. Keep living sent.

[get to know the address]

I am about to state something that is obvious. Maybe so obvious that we don't even think about it. So obvious that we certainly wouldn't think about it in another context besides mail and the post office. You ready? OK. Here goes: Mail goes to an address.

There. I said it. Some people don't like it when you state the obvious because they feel like it is an insult to their intelligence. I didn't intend that at all, I assure you. I hope you didn't take it that way.

I'm just saying that mail doesn't accomplish its purpose without an address. No address, and it's not going anywhere. And if it doesn't go where it is intended to go, it is considered a failure. When this happens, people get really angry at postal workers.

I think we have established that followers of Jesus are letters intended to live sent with God's love and hope to the address of our culture. Whether you think of this metaphor in terms of snail mail or email, letters and emails were both intended to be sent. If we don't go where we are addressed, then we would not be fulfilling our purpose or delivering the message God has written on our hearts. We would not be living as God intended us to live. When this happens, we have no one to be mad at but ourselves.

Are you a letter that is sent or that is sitting? Are you accomplishing your given purpose, or are you purposeless? Where are you going? Are you going at all?

In the next chapter, I am going to look at the "postal route," if you will, where we are sent to deliver. In the chapter that follows, I am going to suggest two reasons why it is important to know where we are going and to actually go where we are addressed. In this chapter, I want to challenge you to get to know your address. Not where you live, like what we expect our kids to know in case they get lost. But where you are being sent—the address for the delivery of the message within you.

[defining contextualization]

I want to unpack a pretty commonly used term—*contextualization*. Bear with me. This is a term that for some people still needs to be defined. So, here goes.

Getting to know the people of the culture we have been sent into and knowing the effective ways to connect with and communicate with them is called contextualization. Now, I am not talking about just learning facts about them. If you study a demographic report on the area in which you live, that doesn't make you an expert on contextualization. You must actually get to know the people. Unless you are befriending them, eating with them, drinking coffee with them, encouraging them, learning from them, and giving yourself away to the people of your culture, you are not contextualizing.

It's like in English class when you are reading a story. You need to know your setting and surroundings and who the characters are. What are these people like? What do they like? Not like? What are their habits? Where do they go? Not go? What are some things they value? What are some things they struggle with? What are perceived issues in their lives? If you don't find the answers to these questions, then you are not learning the context of the story.

In the same way, as followers of Jesus, we must get to know the people we have been sent to if we hope to deliver a message to them. Wouldn't you agree that a message delivered by a friend is always more effective than a message delivered by a stranger?

Besides, Jesus is the King of contextualization. Think about it. He contextualized Moses with Egypt by having him adopted into Pharaoh's family, so that when he returned many years later he knew the scene. He allowed Jonah to be swallowed by a great fish and then spit up, so that he could go preach a message to a people who worshipped a fish god (or so certain scholars say). He asked Hosea to marry a prostitute and stay faithful to her, in order to be contextual with a message of God's faithfulness to Israel, even though they were prostituting themselves in worship to the god Baal. He told fishermen to follow Him and become fishers of men. He delivered a message for the whole world at a time in history when, for the first time, that message could be scattered throughout the world due to an international festival and an international road system. He told the church in Laodicea, a city known for a particular eye medicine and a particular type of clothing, that they needed eye salve to cure their spiritual blindness and new clothes to cover their spiritual nakedness.

If you are still skeptical about Jesus being the King of contextualization, then check out this verse from the Gospel of John, chapter 1, verse 14 (NLT), found in the New Testament of the Bible.

> *So the Word became human and made his home among us. He was full of unfailing love and faithfulness. And we have seen his glory, the glory of the Father's one and only Son.*

Talk about coming to be a friend rather than a disconnected stranger. Jesus, the living Word, who was in the beginning and is God, according to the first verse of that same chapter in John, blew away all the misperceptions of God as being distant. John communicated clearly that He came near. Emmanuel. Probably my favorite Bible word. It means "God with us."

Think about it. How many Americans do researchers say believe there is a God? Lots. If you Google the question you get a range from 82 percent to the mid 90s. So, what's the big deal? They believe there is a God, right?

Well, that there is a God was not the message of Christ. The message of Christ was more than that. Read the Gospels and you find a recurring theme in His teachings. He repeatedly stated that the kingdom is near. His message, in word and in person, was that God is near. His message was not to believe there is a God but to trust in the God who is and who came near.

God came near. Emmanuel. And, people need to hear that, because we live in a context in America today where it does not seem very much like He is near, whether among the churched or the unchurched. What an indictment.

Would it be fair to say that the church has withdrawn from our context, from our culture? Would it be fair to say that the church is not near to our culture? Would it be fair to say that if the church is not near to our culture, if the church is not engaging her context, then the church is not following Jesus? If we don't go to where we have been addressed to go, are we following Him where He intends for us to go?

Jesus is the King of contextualization. John 1:14 could be translated that He "pitched His tent among us." Paul writes in Philippians 2, and I paraphrase, that Jesus did not regard equality with God something to hold on to at all cost, but rather He took off His royal robe and put on human skin to come and be near to us, to walk among us. He came near.

If you follow Jesus, then you are the church. Are you coming near to the culture that Jesus came near to? Are you engaging the context you live in relationally?

What does that mean? Well, it is appropriate to define contextualization in the same way we know Jesus practiced it. We step out of the norms and the privileges that are rightfully ours and we put up a tent in the middle of a culture that other Christians criticize, and we do life with the people of that context. We become their friends, like Jesus told His followers they were to Him. We invite them over. We go to things that mean something to them. We create connection points that enable us to listen and care, not just proselytize.

Contextualization is not accepting cultural norms. That is a common fear and criticism. Contextualization is not being relevant to culture. As one teacher has said, to be relevant means to be behind, and contextualization is about shaping the future, not catching up with the now. Contextualization is not just looking like the people of a context. That's called imitation. Contextualization is not just having events that we think at least 10 percent of our people might bring or at least invite a friend to. That's called an outreach event.

Contextualization is, however, living right in the middle of the culture around us, walking daily in friendship with the people of our particular context, loving them just like they are, living before them in a way that brings out the flavors of God around them and highlights the colors of God around them. It is being a letter they read and say, "Wow. There is a God. He made me and loves me. I want to know Him." Please reread that and then read Matthew 5:13–16. Very similar.

We believe that contextualization is important because coming near is what Jesus did to restore us, and He wasn't afraid to do it. He wasn't afraid we would think He was cool or uncool. He wasn't afraid that He wouldn't know what to talk about or how to hang out. He wasn't concerned that His image might be tarnished if He spent time with people like Matthew and Mary Magdalene and the woman at the well and you and me. He knew He had to come near to deliver a message. He wanted to restore His people to the life they were made for.

If we don't come near, then we fail to deliver that message. We fail to be the letter to culture He intends us to be.

This all comes down to a basic principle: relationships are important to God and important to humanity. As a Christ follower, I should be doing life with both followers and with those who do not follow Jesus. Why? Several reasons.

First, most counselors will tell you that having a group of people you walk with and you are close to and you are supported by is actually extremely important to your emotional, mental, and spiritual health. Second, the health of a church is actually not based on the number who attend but rather the way in which people love one another and are walking relationally in life (Jesus said so in John 13:34–35). Third, the future of the people of our communities depends on the willingness and commitment of the church to walk in relationship with them.

So, how do I contextualize relationship? Bottom line—quit expecting people who don't follow Jesus to come to Him on your terms. Jesus didn't even do this.

Everyone Jesus met, He understood and saw their value as a human being and treated them as such regardless of what was going on in their life. If we are going to live sent contextually, connecting with the lost and going to where we are addressed to go, then we will have to get messy. After all, going deep into the lives of people, meeting them right where they are, can lead us into some muddy waters full of some crazy, sometimes vulgar stuff.

But Jesus did it. He put on skin and walked among us. He got dirty among the very dirt He made and made us with. The problem—His church tends to be spiritual germaphobes.

I heard Chris Seay teaching one time, and he put it this way. Church culture tends to treat culture at large like a public restroom. Think about it. When I go into a public restroom, I try not to touch a thing. I tell my children the same thing when I take them in—"Don't touch anything!" How can we say we follow One who reached out and touched a leper if we aren't willing to engage with those around us in a culture that "Christians" too often condemn as unclean and dangerous or damaging to touch.

The woman at the well, which I've already referenced in a previous chapter, is such a great example of contextualizing relationship. Jesus went out of His way into a town, up to a well, and into a conversation with a Samaritan who was also a woman. She also happened to live in a way that was ugly to some others. Well, Jesus didn't see it that way. He saw a beautiful person, desperate for love, desiring of abundant life, dealing with insecurities about her image and even her God. Jesus discerned this and met her right where she was.

Jesus didn't think His duty was to point out that "Christians don't shack up with people they're not married to, don't you know!" Jesus looked deeper and loved unconditionally. He spoke to all of her concerns, even letting her know that location no longer mattered regarding worship, not Gerazim or Jerusalem but the Spirit within and the truth we follow. The Truth she had given a cup of water to. She probably thought, *What's so different about this guy? Something's so different about what He is saying. It makes sense.* And her life made sense from then on. And then she contextualized relationships and God changed her whole town, probably even the guy she was living with.

[going to where people are matters]

We must stop expecting people to come to us on our terms. We must stop just going to church and commit to go and be the church whenever and wherever. You contextualize relationship when you pitch your tent among the people of your context and befriend them and love them and be there ready to converse with them. Especially be ready when they ask you the question, what's so different about you? But, they won't ask if we don't contextualize relationship. They won't even know to ask unless we actually draw near ourselves.

If we serve the King of contextualization, then we must ask—how are we communicating the gospel into our specific contexts? The message of the gospel doesn't change. How it is stated, framed, or lived out, however, should depend on context. If we love the people we are living as letters to, we will communicate the message written on our hearts to them in such a way that they can connect to it, relate with it, compare it to what they already know and makes sense to them.

[being transparent matters]

Contextualizing relationship is also about complete transparency. It's not about going into a context and befriending people because they should get it together like I have it all together. It's not about being superior and doing something for a bunch of inferiors. I do not have it all together. Neither do you, no matter how much you pretend to.

Why would we want to be seen as having it all together anyway? We don't need to be afraid of people seeing us growing, seeing us as not there yet. If we are really worth something because of what Jesus did rather than because of what I do, then I should want others to see Him in me instead of me in me. I should want to be transparent so that others look through me, success and failures and all, and see Jesus.

Instead of pretending to be super spiritual, what if we were just open and honest about our deep need for Jesus too? Jesus spoke of all of life as spiritual—needing the supernatural to show up to be what it was intended to be. When we see ourselves as worth something only because of what Jesus did, we all are on level ground at the Cross. Every single person. All deeply in need of the love and restoration of Jesus. When we see ourselves in this way, then we are compelled to engage culture, to leave Christian subculture to deliver the message.

Being transparent is about being so honest with others, so transparent, that they see the evidence of what God coming near to me did, and continues to do. It's about living like God's gracious love is my deepest need. It's about them seeing that I am still becoming, still being made every day into what God intended me to be. It's about allowing them to belong just as they are so that they might become what they were intended to be too.

[live sent to where you've been addressed]

Don't forget that God loved us first, even when we were not lovable. He declared us lovable, worth dying for. May we not love and serve others so that we can fulfill our Christian duty or be the good people we too often consider ourselves to be. May we instead love others as letters of God's love, so they can read the message of how He loved them first, just like they are, and how He wants to make their lives abundantly purposeful and meaningful. May we love others so they can become what they were intended to be. That is love, after all, the way Jesus modeled it—to care more about what others are becoming than what I am becoming myself.

[CONSIDER and CONVERSE]

[1]   What is contextualization, and why is it an important element of living sent?

[2]   Think about the context in which you live sent. What are some of the important gathering places for people in the community? Who are some of the key influencers? What are some of the favorite activities of the people you live near and work with?

[3]   John 1:14 pictures Jesus as the King of contextualization. Stop for a moment to pray and thank Jesus for setting the ultimate example of living sent.

[4]   List the three matters suggested in this chapter. Spend some time considering how you can contextualize the gospel more intentionally in your community. Also, spend some time with other followers of Jesus considering the same thing. Then commit to live sent together contextually in your community.

9

stay on the postal route, or wireless travel

(the bulk mail called humanity)

[a story_Bruce]

*B*ruce is a close friend. I had the privilege of coaching both of his boys in basketball. He told me not too long ago of an occasion when living sent to his neighbors became crystal clear.

He and his wife were at a friend's house at a party that was attended mostly by this friend's neighbors. This friend, like Bruce, follows Jesus and lives sent daily. They were casually talking, when Bruce asked his friend, "Who are these folks here I don't know?" His friend responded by telling Bruce who each person was and how he had connected with them. He had served them in some way when they had need, walked with them over time now as a neighbor, and seen a friendship develop. His friend had lived sent to them.

Bruce told me that immediately he had this thought: I am not sure I really know very many of my neighbors' names, if any, and I should.

Bruce is someone who definitely lives sent daily, particularly in the marketplace. But loving his neighbor, living sent to his neighbor, suddenly came into clear view as overdue.

Are you living sent to your neighbors?

[spheres of influence]

*W*as it 1992? Something like that. Wait, let me Google it . . . Wow! Assuming my online research is accurate, here's a quick look at the evolution of email:

Email started in the mid 1960s and early email addresses had to specify a path (ie, exactly which machine a message was going to travel on to get from the sender to the receiver).

> Messages were often lost and could take as long as a week to reach their destination. In 1971 the @ symbol was chosen to combine the user and host name (i.e., username@host). In the 1980s this was extended to include the domain (i.e., username@hostdomain). This standard for email remains today.
>
> The year 1988 saw the first authorized use of commercial email on the Internet. In 1989 the CompuServe mail system was connected through the Ohio State University network. In 1993 AOL connected their system to the Internet and email became global.

Seriously? The 1960s? It makes sense, I guess. I actually have a friend whose wife worked on the original supercomputer. Maybe she had one of the first email addresses.

Maybe you really dig the 1950s. Before email. If so, then don't think of the live sent metaphor in terms of email. Think of it in terms of what email people call snail mail—the slow version of sending a letter through post office and postal workers.

That's why I titled this chapter "stay on the postal route (or 'wireless travel')." If you like snail mail, then live sent daily on the postal route. If you like email, then live sent daily wirelessly (everywhere). If you like Twitter or Facebook, just consider them an advanced form of wireless travel.

What's the point? As letters of God's love sent into the address of our culture, we must live sent daily everywhere and at all times in the midst of our spheres of influence.

What are those spheres? What's the postal route? Where will we travel wirelessly?

[family]

The primary sphere of influence in all of our daily lives is our family. This sphere includes mom and dad and siblings. It includes spouse and kids. It includes grandparents. It includes uncles and aunts and cousins. It includes stepkids. Those to whom you should always relate, because they are biologically or maritally connected with you.

Living sent to family is not always easy. I don't know exactly why that is, but I can say that familiarity tends to breed elevated tension or apathetic complacency. An example of elevated tension would be those two brothers who can trigger an argument with each other in no time over the slightest issues, and at the top of the list is religion and politics. An example of apathetic complacency would be that husband who has convinced himself that he works so hard all day to be the breadwinner that he doesn't need to focus energy and attention on his wife and kids when he gets home. He's worked hard enough that day. Besides, his wife and kids will always love him and be there, right? Who needs to cultivate those relationships? Again, at the risk of stating the obvious, cultivating family relationships needs to be a priority. It just makes sense that if you are your neighbor's best friend but neglect your spouse and/or kids, you are not a legitimate letter anymore, because the people closest to you to whom you are most familiar see you as a phony.

[neighbor]

Speaking of living sent to your neighbor—that is the second sphere of influence for daily living. And Jesus thought it was a very valuable one. In fact, when asked what the most important commandments were, He listed two relational commands—love God and love your neighbor. He said everything else hangs on these two.

I have already mentioned in a previous chapter the story known as the parable of the good Samaritan, but let's discuss it here again for the sake of illustration. One guy asked Jesus, "Who is my neighbor?" He asked this in an attempt to justify not loving the people he couldn't stand to love, the people he's been conditioned to have prejudiced feelings toward, the people who just simply got under his skin.

Jesus told a story of a Jewish man robbed and beaten and left for dead. Two religious leaders came along the road, saw him, and passed by, excusing themselves with the customs and rules they had to uphold because of their prominent positions as religious leaders. But then a Samaritan came along.

Of the neighboring ethnic group to the Jews in that day. And they didn't like them. In fact, when Jesus told the story, it is guaranteed that people became uncomfortable even when He mentioned the word *Samaritan*. That Samaritan guy, whom most Jews would never help, in Jesus' story helped a Jew. Even went above and beyond, paying for his medical care and lodging, and promising to pay more if need be.

Then, Jesus asked the guy who originally asked the question:

"What do you think? Which of the three became a neighbor to the man attacked by robbers?" "The one who treated him kindly," the religion scholar responded. Jesus said, "Go and do the same."

—Luke 10:36–37 (*The Message*)

I am constantly amazed at how overlooked the importance of kindness is. Talk about stating the obvious. Jesus wasn't just talking about handing out tracts or knocking on doors here. Not that those are all bad. He was emphasizing our need to stop and connect with and get to know the people around us who may be in need. We would never know if they were hurting or lonely or broken or beaten up inside. The needs we see most often go unnoticed because they are not as obvious as being beaten up on the side of the road, but they are as significant a need, nonetheless.

Jesus was simply talking about being kind to the people around us, especially when they are in need. Paul said in the letter to the Roman church that God's kindness leads people to repentance. So, kindness must be a pretty important component of God's message that we carry in our hearts.

And how often does the church (the people who follow Jesus together) go to church, while backing out of their driveways, clicking down their garages, and passing by their neighbors whom they hardly even know? What if they made a slight change? Maybe fewer church activities on their schedule and a lot more of being the church in the midst of whatever their schedule already is. Why add church to what you do when you can be the church in all you do?

Seriously, this is a big deal here. The church passes by the very people we should be connecting with, befriending, encouraging, caring for—our neighbors—for the sake of going to do church stuff with other churchgoers.

stay on the postal route

The problem is simple—people go to church too much and are not being the church enough.

We must live sent to our neighbors.

[marketplace]

The next basic sphere of influence in our daily living is the marketplace. And what a significant sphere it is. People who follow Jesus spend anywhere from 60 to 80 hours per week in the marketplace, if not more. At work. At the grocery store. At the mall. At a restaurant. At the mechanic. At the coffee shop. In a carpool. At school. The list could go on. If people who follow Jesus spend so much of the 168 hours of their week there, then that means that the church exists in the marketplace more time each week than any other sphere of living.

Stop and think about that.

Are you being the church in the marketplace? Do you live sent to the people you work with, go to school with, are served by in the marketplace? If not, then are we failing to arrive at one of the more prominent destinations (the people in the marketplace) to which we have been addressed as God's letters?

When you see a co-worker who clearly has hurt in her eyes, do you stop and ask her how she is really doing, or is it just the token "How are you?" that has become an insincere greeting in our culture? Do you listen? Do you express concern? If the Holy Spirit prompts you to encourage your co-workers or speak words of challenge or direction to them, do you take the time? Or are you complaining about your job so much, so self-focused, that you don't even notice those around you who might need a letter of love and hope from the God who made them?

My friend Jamie has a master's degree in accounting but also sees himself as a "pastor to the marketplace." Jamie told me once that living sent in the marketplace is not just about being known as moral and ethical. Being moral in marketplace dealings is actually a good thing, especially in today's currency. Being a guy who makes right choices and wants to be known as a guy who makes right choices is one thing. But it's not living sent. Living sent in the marketplace would actually be about loving the people you work with, with a genuine love, that causes them to look deeper to the source of that love.

Furthermore, are we so consumed with filling roles for Sunday morning church stuff that we forget about the majority of time lived as the church? As a pastor, I admit that some culpability falls to the pastors of our churches. We have expected people to fill slots for Sunday morning ministry and marketed to followers to entice them to join our dreams of more prominent church gatherings. We have had this Sunday morning emphasis so much that people aren't reminded or challenged or encouraged to live sent daily in the marketplace.

I have spoken to many marketplace leaders, many businesspeople, who have told me in various forms that they are tired of pastors and church leaders using brilliant executives and managers and workers to hand out Sunday morning handouts rather than equipping them to love and walk with their co-workers. The value of ten marketplace leaders living sent is exponentially greater than the value of what the pastor has to say at a gathering.

Now, don't misread that! I know how pastors are. I am one. We get all worked up with our fragile egos when people question the importance of the stuff we do. But let's learn from the Master here. He Himself said that His followers would do greater things than He did (John 14). What?! Greater than Jesus? What did He mean?

I can only guess that at least one of His implications was that He was one man, while His followers were many. And He was focused on one task—fulfilling the restorative work of a gracious God who gave His life to redeem the world. His followers had many tasks, all wrapped up in one purpose—to send the message that God had come near to restore us into full relationship with Himself and to give us abundant life as was intended. The pastor is one person. Those who live in the marketplace are many.

I did not say that pastors teaching the Bible is unimportant. It is. But the impact of preaching and teaching the Scriptures is lost if the hope is to bring listeners back the next Sunday. The goal of our gatherings must not just be to come and see, but rather to go and be. To live sent daily among the people that we work with and are served by and go to school with in the marketplace.

If you are not living sent in the marketplace, assess your commitment to follow Jesus. If you are not living sent in the marketplace, then you are wasting more than 50 percent of your awake time each week (assuming you sleep an average of 6 hours a night and spend at least 70 hours a week in the marketplace). That should wake us up to realize the story of the church is far greater than what happens on Sunday morning.

[world]

*A*nother basic sphere of influence for daily living is the world. Better said, local and global community. In the past, church culture too often has emphasized this sphere through disconnected, scheduled service projects in our local community or state and international missions trips to far-off places. There is nothing wrong with local service projects and missions trips. But I would suggest that living sent to our world isn't just about a get-in then get-out experience.

We have witnessed the significance of ongoing relationship through focused relational service. In fact, I encourage you to consider focusing your living sent to the world to one local element and one global element. There is so much need out there, it can be overwhelming. But if you focus relationally with someone locally and globally for an ongoing period of time, you will discover how rich the friendships and transformation can be, for both those serving and being served.

Josh and Kelly decided to do this locally. They went to a local community center in an impoverished area of town that was on their heart. They asked if they could provide afterschool food and activities for the kids there. From providing a meal to exercise classes to a tea party for girls to simply playing football with the boys, they lived sent to their world locally and they keep going back. The impact has been significant.

Chad and Cindy decided to do this globally. We had been emphasizing the need to be willing to give up everything for those whom Christ loves but who are often ignored. They literally did it. Chad gave up his prize BMW, selling it and giving the proceeds to help an orphanage and school in a village near Awassa, Ethiopia. They are also helping to build a well to provide clean water for the villagers. And they will be going there soon and will keep going.

One suggestion. Josh and Kelly and Chad and Cindy aren't doing this alone. They have invited others to do it with them. Living sent to our world together is such a beautiful way to share the letter of God's near love.

[Web]

The final sphere of influence for daily living in today's world is living sent online—the Web. You might say, "All I do online, when I even go online, is check my bank statement and answer email." Well, that's a start.

What if you have to call customer service for your bank? What if, just for that one instance, the customer service rep needs to be the one served? You hear in her voice a loneliness that reminds you of a difficult season that you drudged through. You sense the Spirit say, "Ask her how she is. Then ask her how she really is. Tell her you can hear it in her voice. Then listen for Me to tell you what to say and do."

Emails are letters themselves. Letters change lives. What if God's Spirit prompts you to send an email to someone to encourage them? What if someone has been on your mind? What if that's been God's Spirit keeping them on your mind? You don't know why. You just know that you keep thinking about them. So you email them. And when they respond, you find out why they've been on your mind. They unload a torrent of hopelessness, and God opens the opportunity for you to be a letter of refreshing, cool water for them to drink.

Those are just two examples of living sent online. But there are more consistent, relational ways too. Twitter. Facebook. MySpace. Chat rooms.

I can't prove what I am about to say. It's just my look-around-online kind of survey. But I have noticed that when people are sharing online, emotions and thoughts flow more freely and more authentically. Probably because they don't have a physical insecurity to overcome. They can crop their avatar (little picture that identifies them) to show what they want, if they even have one. There's no physical prettiness or ugliness to overcome. They are simply themselves. And in those social online networking tools that are so popular at the moment, the opportunity to genuinely befriend and profoundly deliver a message of love and hope is huge. Don't miss it.

Live sent online.

stay on the postal route

OK. Those were the spheres of influence for daily living. Our postal route as letters. Our wireless travel as emails. In the next chapter, I want to suggest two reasons why we need to know to whom and to where we are addressed.

[CONSIDER and CONVERSE]

The author writes in this chapter:

> *"As letters of God's love sent into the address of our culture, we must live sent daily everywhere and at all times in the midst of our spheres of influence."*

He then goes on to describe five spheres of influence. Commit to pray over the next month for at least one person you connect with or at least encounter in each of the five spheres of influence of your daily life. Then, consider spending time with other followers of Jesus with whom you do life and think together about ways you can live sent more intentionally in each of the five spheres.

[1] Family

[2] Neighbor

[3] Marketplace

[4] World

[5] Web

10

learn and live the ways of the author

(discipling instead of discipleship,
or "letters beget letters")

[a story_Fiona]

*F*iona is five and three-quarters years old (that three-quarters is a really big deal). You probably remember when it was too. She is from Scotland. Her family vacations in central Florida about 16 weeks per year. Her dad's job allows them to travel like that.

One of her school friends doesn't follow Jesus, and neither do the friend's parents. Fiona and her parents don't see Jesus as a religious alternative, but as the Giver of abundant life. Who wouldn't want that? Fiona is not afraid to share about God's goodness and love. And she has piqued the curiosity of her schoolmate.

So much so that her schoolmate's parents asked about it. When out to dinner with Fiona's parents one night, they spoke of a recent event their daughters had been a part of together. In the Magic Kingdom at Walt Disney World, the two girls enjoyed a makeover at the Bibbity Bobbity Boutique. Afterward, Fiona's friend declared to her parents, "I have achieved everything in my life, perhaps except seeing God." She is six.

Fiona's parents assumed their daughter's friend had picked this God thought up at school in Scotland where both girls attend. It is a school where a Christ-centered example is still set.

A great conversation ensued. Fiona's dad, curious about what provoked the interest, asked where this remark about seeing God had come from. The schoolmate's parents responded, "It is Fiona. She's been talking about it with our daughter, who then asked us about it. So, we wanted to ask you."

All along, Fiona's parents, who love these people very much, had been trying to find their "moment" and the right words to share about the abundant life they have in Jesus. And here it was. All because of Fiona.

A six-year-old (actually a quarter away). A letter from God. Alive and delivering an intriguing message with her actions and her words. Did I mention that she's nearly six?

[discipling instead of discipleship]

The Author may not be a term you have ever used for God. I consider it an appropriate metaphor, though. After all, the passages we have highlighted in this book from 2 Corinthians, along with others, describe God as having written a message to us. Therefore, He would be the Author of our lives and of the letter He has written on our hearts.

I really appreciate great authors. I pay attention to how they write, how they communicate, how they describe. The best ones can not only tell you something, they can take you there. Get you right in the middle of the story.

God does that for us. In fact, He entered into His-Story (history) to show us life as He intended. A sent life.

Jesus' last words were to His followers, and His message was clear—as you are going, make disciples. As you will see in this chapter, discipling is all about learning. And who better to learn from than the Author Himself?

[is it discipleship or is it making disciples?]

There may be some confusion, though, in church culture about discipling. I think this is because we have created a thing called discipleship and emphasized it instead of exemplifying and emphasizing discipling.

What is discipleship anyway? A local church family in our community branded their whole children's ministry area as a ship called the Disciple Ship. Pretty cool looking and well thought out and hokey-corny all at the same time. There are a lot of church families who still set aside a night a week for what used to be called discipleship training. Various names describe this time. Didactic teaching defines it. Unfortunately, this kind of thinking is epidemic among church culture in the US.

We have made the Great Commission given to us from Jesus into nothing more than a program we can package and sell and pull off in two hours or less on a Sunday or Wednesday. This is not discipleship.

So, what is it? Well, technically speaking, the word *discipleship* doesn't even exist in the Scriptures. In fact, the word itself implies a programmed sort of approach, participation in something we know we should participate in but would feel better about our participation in it if we actually had a program that applauded our accomplishment in that area. Kind of like

learn and live the ways of the author

bipartisanship and fellowship and sportsmanship. All three are important and necessary, but all three have programmed emphases that supposedly help people do what they should simply be doing naturally because it is that important.

You might say, "That's semantics." No it isn't. Language is important, and if we want something to be more than a program, if we want something to be more about process, then we need to emphasize it in our language. Jesus did.

He spoke of discipleship not in terms of discipleship, but in terms of discipling. As you are going, make disciples. The participle phrase "as you are going" combined with the command to make disciples implies process. An ongoing emphasis is there when you see that suffix ing on a word. And it matters because it matters enough to be doing it and to keep doing it.

And it has always been the central purpose of followers of Jesus. As much as it may hurt some people's feelings, the Great Commission is not entirely lived out via missions and evangelism. Jesus described missions as serving anyone and everyone every day, not just once a year. And, Jesus never divided the concepts we call evangelism and discipleship. In fact, He seemed to speak of the two as parts of the same process. He called that process discipling. And He said that "as we go" in everyday life (not just "go" programmatically or scheduled), we should be discipling.

[so what is discipling?]

So, what is it? I want to suggest this basic definition that I believe has profound implication in all of my daily living.

> Discipling is learning and living the ways of Jesus so that others learn and live His ways, too, so that others learn and live His ways, too, and so on

Discipling is all about proclaiming the message that God has come near, mainly by living like He actually did. As we live His ways, we show His love by how we come near as a friend to the people around us every day, not only through some service project. That's how other disciples are made—they catch it as we do life with them.

Thus, it is a process. However, it is not and must not be simply a linear process. It is instead a very fluid, ongoing process. It must not just be about basic assimilation. I fear that plugging every church visitor into some program so they can learn "how we do church around here" has become the goal of discipling for many church families. Membership classes can be helpful in certain contexts. Don't get me wrong. I am simply suggesting that kind of programmed emphasis has too often left us with two very unhealthy results.

First, an assimilation emphasis often results in an end of a discipling program rather than a beginning of an ongoing discipling process. Leaders too often give energy to this program rather than to equipping and releasing multiple followers. Programs typically have a beginning and end (although some church families like to keep programs going long after they should have ended). In contrast, an ongoing discipling process is indicative of a never-ending movement. It results in people not only being disciples, but also being released to become disciplers. Those released then engage and disciple multiple friends and hopefully followers to also do the same, and so on.

Second, in that programmed emphasis, we have created processes that have in turn created what I will call an imaginary readiness line. When Jesus said, "Come follow Me," He did not then say, "and take these four classes so that you shall be ready to be a leader and lead others unto Me." This has become an unintentional result of this programmed approach, and has thus resulted in somewhat sterile and timid followers who think they need more classes to learn what to say or what to do right so people can "get right" with God. This is not healthy.

Jesus taught His followers over time. He did this in the middle of relationship with them. He did this in the middle of a process that allowed them to learn and live, to be served and to serve, to have both theory and practice. He released them to connect and engage and learn and live and lead others to Him immediately. It is easy then to conclude that discipling is a process which has as its core value the necessity of doing life together.

Since there is not a set process, or at least I am suggesting as such, then what is the process like?

[the elements of the ongoing, never-ending process]

I would suggest three elements. These three do not flow from A to Z. They ebb and flow. Each may be involved at any one time, while all may be involved at any one time. It's kind of fluid like that, kind of messy like that, kind of unpredictable like that. Kind of like doing life together.

The first element I would suggest for the discipling process is relationship. Every aspect of learning the ways of Jesus and living the ways of Jesus is both validated and authenticated inside relationship. We were made for togetherness. We are stifled when we are alone. The church is people following Jesus together, not an individual. Relationship is paramount. Discussing the teachings of Jesus requires relationship. In fact, I have seen so often that true transformation happens in the midst of ongoing relational dialogue. That's evident in the discipling process for those who walked face-to-face with Jesus.

Accountability for living out the teachings of Jesus requires relationship. Our culture pretends that hierarchical structures encapsulate accountability, but forced or enforced accountability is not true accountability at all. When I do something for someone because I have to rather than because I want to, or when I am motivated by obligation rather than love, that is not accountability as described in the New Testament. It is not based in reciprocal relationship. It is not based in love. It is not based in common purpose with the goal of unified restoration and growth. It is, you do something for me or you are fired or don't get paid, etc. Accountability doesn't really exist, at least as modeled by Jesus and described in the New Testament, apart from relationship.

Multiplicative results for discipling cannot happen without relationship. Multiplication in the literal sense, being fruitful and multiplying, can only happen within relationship. In the figurative sense, the necessity for relationship is the same. If we are to see disciples made, then we must engage people in genuine friendship. Multiplication cannot be programmed. It happens. It blossoms. It is a product of relationships that flourish and have purpose.

When we befriend someone, our agenda must be more than just adding them to our church membership. Rather, we should walk with them in such a way that they taste and see the love of Jesus, that they witness His ways lived out, and that they learn His ways and follow. This multiplication becomes exponential when it is not constrained by programming standards. It becomes exponential when relationship allows it the freedom to blossom.

The second element I would suggest for the discipling process is discernment. Unfortunately, this element of discipling is often left out within programmed discipleship. Discerning where someone is spiritually and where someone is going in life is not required in programmed discipleship. You can simply plug someone into the linear process. Problem is, what results is a stifled disciple, which is actually an oxymoron. Let me explain.

As followers of Jesus, we have the Holy Spirit residing within us. Jesus spoke of the many ways having the Holy Spirit matters in the daily life of a follower as recorded in John 14 to 16. Paul follows that with some pretty insightful teaching in 1 Corinthians and Ephesians. John also elaborates on it in 1 John 5. Among the many aspects of what the Spirit does in and through us is discernment.

As we engage people in relationship, we need to do more than think, *What are the five steps I must take this person through so they will now be a disciple?* Maybe a better approach would be to pray something like this:

> Holy Spirit, please give me discernment into the heart and life of my new friend. Give me Your wisdom and insight so that I may know how to love them right where they are and encourage them for where You want them to go as we walk on this mutual journey with You.

What if we prayed that? Don't you think the Spirit would grant us discernment? Then, we would be pulled into an amazing adventure of learning the ways of Jesus and living out those ways alongside someone into whose life we are speaking encouragement and direction as the Holy Spirit leads us. If we would listen as the Spirit provides this discernment, we would be able to determine where on the journey a person is rather than pigeonholing them or trying to take them through a step-by-step process.

This is important. Think about it. When is the last time you met someone at point A? Anyone besides a child born to you? If we discount where someone has already been in their lives, we will miss out on ways God has already been at work in a person's life before we ever met them. Jesus took this seriously. With Peter, Matthew, Mary, Nicodemus, the woman at the well. We must take it seriously too. It is important for us to realize that discipleship is not a program that begins after someone begins to follow Jesus. It is a process that even begins before conversion. You can't argue with that principle either, because a cursory reading of the four Gospels makes it plain. Jesus invited 12 guys into relationship and entered into a journey with them that God the Father had already been walking on with them. In other words, He had already been at work. He was there through the tragedy and victories of their lives previous to their encounter with Jesus. Now, Jesus was going to complete the work that had been begun and continue it toward more and more completion—the discipling process that never ends.

And in that relationship, Jesus discerned where each one was on his journey. It is important that we do the same. God's Spirit can enable us and pull us into an amazing life-transforming and life-restoring process at the same time, both for the person we are walking with and for ourselves.

Discernment also is more important than degrees and training. The Spirit can make the uneducated become wise. Thank God for that because it means I am eligible to be a discipler just like you are eligible. The point is, anyone can do it. Any one of us can listen to God's Spirit leading us to walk in relationship with others and learn/teach the ways of Jesus and live those ways alongside them.

Bottom line with discernment. If we take this element out of the discipling process and simply plug people into discipleship programs, then we must be OK reaping what we sow. That is, we must be OK with producing stifled disciplers who equate discipling with getting more people into the program. We will reap programmed disciples looking for the next program rather than active disciplers looking for the next relationship. Instead, we must sow in such a way that we reap followers who experience the beauty and richness of God's Spirit revealing insight to them and allowing them to be a part of discerning where a person has been and where God is taking them.

The third element of discipling I would suggest is release. I believe it is safe to say that for the most part, church culture has made discipleship more about retention than release. People are encouraged to stay in discipleship programs rather than being released to actually disciple. Church gurus stress our need to grow the church, and what they mean is more people in gathering and in small groups. I would suggest that Jesus wants to grow His church out there among the harvest, not in here among those already harvested. The harvest grows out there.

The third element of discipling I would suggest is release. A disciple of Jesus will be seen discipling in the middle of culture, or he or she is no disciple at all. A follower will be fishing, I once heard it said, or he or she is not a follower at all. And fishing is not just about evangelism. Again, Jesus never separated these two concepts. Discipling is fishing. Learning the ways of Jesus and living those ways so that others learn and live them so that others learn and live them and so on. And that happens out there where disciples are released to disciple.

Discipling is more than some class once a week that we market and hope for high attendance. It is learning and living all week. It is eating together. It is praying together. It is having fun together. It is doing things of interest together. It is serving together. It is doing life together.

That is the model of discipling that we were given by Jesus, but to make it easier on ourselves, we boiled it down to a formula and program and said, "Go through this class, and you will be disciples."

It's not that classes aren't important. It's not that gathering together in classes or for collective worship is not important. It's not that we don't need to have Bible study together. These are important, but these can't be the extent of our discipling.

On the first night our church family gathered as a core group, we shared four statements with those who gathered. One of them was this—we will not busy you with church activities, but rather we will equip and release you to be the church within your daily and weekly activities. This is a must if we hope for followers of Jesus to actually engage culture and see others begin to follow Jesus.

Learn and live the ways of the author

If we stay intent on discipleship as a program, then we will continue to very effectively produce absorbers of Jesus knowledge. This would be unfortunate, because we will continue to be very ineffective at making what Jesus asked us to make. Making more intelligent Christians is not the goal of this process. In fact, we have intellectualized and bulletized the message of Christ so much that culture no longer sees it as spiritually vital, as alive.

A key aspect to understand here is this—truth is not a concept we learn in a classroom but a Person we relate to Who changes every portion of our lives. If we do not emphasize release as a key element of discipling, then our culture will not encounter the Person whom those released are following. In fact, they might not encounter anything of Jesus at all, since His supposed followers will only be entrenched in discipleship classrooms rather than being out among the people Jesus died for.

Some good closing questions might be: What would be the evidence that this kind of discipling process is working? Would it be people enrolled in another discipleship class, or people engaged in relationships within culture? Would it be people moving on toward the next step in a discipleship program, or people listening to the Spirit within them, involving them in an ongoing, personal journey in which God has been on the move already? Would it be programs grown and people retained or people released so that the church grows out where Jesus wants it to grow?

Let's surrender our programs and enter into this relational releasing process known as discipling and see what happens. Let's live sent daily and be discipling. If we will, then we will be intentionally delivering a message, learning and living the ways of the Author, and giving other people the opportunity to see the Author in our ways. Then, they will learn and begin to live His ways too. Then, we will be discipling.

[CONSIDER and CONVERSE]

[1] What is the difference between discipleship and discipling?

[2] A basic definition of discipling is suggested. Do you agree with this

definition and agree with the importance of discipling?
Why or why not?

[3] Reflect on the three elements of discipling suggested in this chapter. Consider how these three elements can be carried out in your five spheres of life (family, neighbors, marketplace, world, Web). Take the time to discuss these with other followers of Jesus with whom you do life.

[4] Read over the questions the author presents in the second to last paragraph of the chapter. Ask for the Holy Spirit to help you turn these responses into an "as you go" process.

11

neither snow, nor rain, nor heat, nor gloom of night...

(safety can't be a prerequisite for living sent)

[a story_Josh]

*J*osh is the general manager of House Blend Cafe in Ocoee, Florida (houseblendcafe.com). His employees serve more than gourmet coffee and delicious food and great desserts. They serve their community. Josh considers himself a pastor in the marketplace and a pastor to his community. House Blend Cafe exists as a for-profit business that tries to make a profit in order to give it away into its community. And Josh is the heart and soul of the cafe.

Every customer is served and loved in more ways than one. Josh hears comments frequently that the spirit customers sense in the cafe is very different from other coffeehouses and cafes. Because it is.

Josh is living sent to them. In fact, a group of the café's customers now meet regularly with Josh not only to discuss the ways of Jesus but to also live them out together as they serve in the local community. They are giving themselves away together in the heart of one of the most impoverished and dangerous areas of town.

Several years ago, Josh was deeply disturbed when a patron of the cafe, a homeless man who lived in the woods across the street from the cafe, was murdered by a local teen. Josh had fed the man several times. He admitted, though, that when he came in, it was generally during heavy rush times and Josh didn't give him the attention he deserved.

I will never forget the words Josh uttered when he was sharing his heartache with me about the senseless murder of this man. "Why didn't I ever cross the street? I should have crossed the street. I assure you that from now on, I will be crossing the street."

And he does. Even into an area many people consider dangerous. A friend of Josh's recently decided to join Josh and his group for a movie night that they do to connect and cultivate togetherness in that community. The friend asked, "Will we have security or at least notify the police?"

Living sent isn't safe. But Josh and his family do know the One whose love and nearness make them secure.

[endurance required]

Did you know that the United States Postal Service (USPS) does not actually have an official slogan? I did not know that. Until now. And now you do too. The USPS does not have an official slogan.

The unofficial slogan, though, is one you've probably heard in some form or another. The original saying is attributed to the Greek historian Herodotus around 500 B.C. as he referred to the Persian mounted postal couriers he observed during the war between the Greeks and Persians. He is said to have uttered, "Neither snow, nor rain, nor heat, nor gloom of night stays these courageous couriers from the swift completion of their appointed rounds." This saying became identified with the USPS when, in the late 1800s, it was engraved on the outside of the New York City General Post Office building.

Pretty interesting. It sounds like the resolve of letter carriers has been strong for quite some time, even before the war between dogs and postal workers began. It also sounds like these early postal carriers from back in the day of the war between Greeks and Persians had less concern for safety and more concern for their mission.

I hope the same can be said of those of us commissioned to live sent. Unfortunately, in church culture, safety seems to be more important than mission. I say this, because people who call themselves Christians tend to withdraw from culture more than engage. We don't want our kids to get "stained by the world" or be corrupted like the people in our culture. Personal safety becomes more important than those persons in our culture who need to read God's letter.

As Paul wrote in Romans 10, how will they ever read that letter unless we walk among them? Unless our feet take us there. Unless the very hearts on which the message has been written are filled with compassion rather than fear, concern rather than desire for comfort.

The fact is, we serve a God who not only is not safe, but who also did not play it safe.

neither snow, nor rain, nor heat, nor gloom of night...

[God is not safe]

How is God not safe? Well, read the Scriptures. Safety does not seem to be the main concern of God for His people. Too often, people die or are hurt both in the midst of God's mission advancing and as consequences of evil people acting against God's people. Jesus Himself said that those who follow Him will not be safe in this world. The world will hate us, as Jesus was hated. And people who followed God in the Scriptures, well frankly, many of them died.

How is that safe?

It is a common cliché in Christian subculture, but I am afraid that it is a very deceptive statement. It is simply not true. People say, "The safest place to be is in the center of God's will." That is a lie. It is not safe in the center of God's will.

While there are those who are protected while boldly standing for God (i.e., Daniel and his three fiery friends from the Book of Daniel in the Old Testament), there are many, many more who are not protected while living out His purposes. Was it safe to be Joseph? I mean, he ended up with a great gig, but he went through major turmoil to get there. Was it safe to be Job? Again, great in the end. But never disregard hurt remembered. Pain is not forgotten just because people and things have been replaced. Was it safe to be Elijah? Running for his life from prophets and kings and queens who wanted his head? Was it safe to be Jeremiah? Given a message and winding up a slave in Egypt? There are a lot more. All of these you can read more about in the Old Testament of the Bible.

So, what about the New Testament of the Bible? Was it safe to be John the Baptist? Ask the one who chopped off his head. Was it safe to be Stephen? Jesus definitely noticed his present danger, even stood up to watch him be stoned. And did nothing to stop it. Was it safe to be those early disciples, so many of whom lost their lives for the sake of the message Jesus gave them to deliver, the letter He called them to be?

These were all people who some might say were in the center of God's will, and they were not safe.

What about today? What about Steven Curtis Chapman? His lyrics and music have been used of God to change multiple lives. He lost his five-year-old adopted daughter because she was run over accidentally by his teenage son in their driveway. What about my friend Rick? On his way to worship gathering one Sunday morning, his family was blindsided by a vehicle and his daughter killed. What about my friends Rick and Laurie? While they were serving overseas in West Africa, Laurie was personally attacked. A few years later, two of their children were caught in the middle of a gun battle at a boarding school during an attempted coup.

What about my mom and dad? Serving Jesus and loving people selflessly for almost 50 years, and then one night they were run over by a car in a New Orleans crosswalk. Dad broken with multiple fractures. Mom debilitated with a traumatic brain injury. She died four months later in the hospital as a result. How are these safe?

In the meantime, persecution of the church across the world continues in graver fashion than ever.

It is safe to conclude that God is not safe. Following Him is no guarantee of safety and protection, and any preacher who sells you a prosperity message claiming safety and favor if you follow Jesus is simply a liar.

Mr. Beaver, in C. S. Lewis's "Chronicles of Narnia" books, said it best. When asked by Susan if Aslan was safe, Mr. Beaver responded: "Course he isn't safe. But he's good."

Another famous line from the same collection of stories: "People who have not been in Narnia sometimes think that a thing cannot be good and terrible at the same time."

The Cross is a great example. The most terrible form of death known to man at the time of Jesus' death, and yet the goodness of the Cross is the hope in which we stand. Not safe, but good. Terrible and good all at the same time.

People tend to equate difficult with bad, but that is not always the case. If we believe God to be good, if we can trust Him as the One who ultimately desires good for us, then we must believe in Him steadfastly and stay resolute in our commitment to be His letter no matter our circumstance. We either actually believe that He is good and can work all things together for the good for those who love Him, or we don't.

Simply stated, God is not safe. And those who follow Him will not be guaranteed safety either. So, we must quit playing it safe, retreating from the very culture around us to whom God has sent us as His letter, and boldly and resolutely live sent daily smack-dab in the middle of the world God so loved.

neither snow, nor rain, nor heat, nor gloom of night...

[God did not play it safe]

I like to encourage people that God does not ask us to do what He has not already done Himself. The same is true of His call on our lives to be His letter. He Himself became a letter. John called Him the Word. A living Word was Jesus, embodying the very message God had been communicating all along and continues to communicate to us today. We today are that embodiment, as followers of Jesus. And Jesus did not play it safe.

How much do I even need to type here to illustrate this point? Jesus spent time with the scorned of society, argued with priests, touched lepers, and told his betrayer to carry on with his task. Then, when given chances to save himself from the most painful death the government could guarantee, he passed. You see clearly that God did not play it safe. He Himself lost His Son who lost His life for the mission to restore us. The movie "The Passion" captured very well how unsafe it really was for Jesus. If you have not seen it, beware. It may illustrate this point more than you wanted it to.

We carry on that same mission today, as His letters. And we must. May we grow in our commitment and resolve. May we surrender our fears. May we engage the people of our culture around us, not retreat. May we be genuine friends to people who are not just like us. May we live sent.

And may "neither snow, nor rain, nor heat, nor gloom of night stay these courageous couriers from the swift completion of their appointed rounds" as letters from the God who loves us and who did not play it safe.

You might be wondering how can we make it through this life following a God who says He loves us in the midst of this lack of safety. Well, I don't actually know the full answer to that. But here is a bit of what I learned during a very unsafe period in my own life when my mom and dad were recovering from getting hit by an SUV while walking after dinner on a business trip to New Orleans. I hope it will encourage you to at least trust and walk with resolve as you live sent.

[mom's new shoes]

It was raining when the plane landed. A storm had blown through the New Orleans area that morning, and my flight arrived at 9:15 a.m. The weekend with my family in Orlando had been sky blue. Seeing Jen and the kids and our church family meant more than I can express in written words. Very refreshing. But not this morning. I was reentering the nightmare that took me away for my wife and kids for over four months. This particular morning was all grey. And my heart was too. It really hit me hard what had happened to Mom and Dad that had changed all of our lives.

When I arrived, text messaging revealed that Dad was in therapy, so I headed across the river to see Mom. I was looking forward to another half-smile and those beautiful, open, brown eyes. And that's what I saw. Very thankful. I spent some time with her, asking yes and no questions, reading notes from Caring Bridge, and talking with the medical staff. Then, I headed to see Dad.

We went for a walk. I pushed his wheelchair outside to a windy spot under the breezeway, grabbed a chair for myself, and we sat together. I summarized for him what I had taught Sunday morning in our worship gathering back home. It sparked deeper interaction, especially because we are walking through 1 John right now. One of Dad's favorites.

Then, I read him some of the notes from Caring Bridge. Without fail, each note carved a canyon from his heart that expressed itself through tears of joy. I asked him, "Pop, do you know how lucky you are? How many people get to hear the impact of their lives before they die?"

My father-in-law and I had talked about that the previous Saturday night. We wondered why we usually wait to share how much someone really means to us until after they can no longer hear us.

I headed back to see Mom. She wasn't tracking with the clarity that I had seen the week before. She seemed kind of out of it. She seemed tired. I thought, *What do I expect? There will be good days and bad days.*

"You have to take this month-to-month now. This will be a two-year process. We won't be able to say, with confidence, where she will really return to until that time."

Those were the words of the neurosurgeon from Orlando who had performed my neck surgery in 2007. I had called him to get counsel on Mom—about her care and about transferring her back to Orlando. We were working on logistics for both her and Dad to transfer to Orlando, mainly to get Mom into a brain center there that had been highly recommended to us.

neither snow, nor rain, nor heat, nor gloom of night...

Two years. It's amazing how a two-second accident can change the next two years of Mom's life. And ours.

I'm just being honest with you. My heart was so heavy and gray. I thought, how do people make it through stuff like this—hard stuff when loved ones are impacted—without Jesus?

How do people make it? How do they make it apart from the nearness of His love? How do they have the resolve?

I believe that He loves us, you know. That's why there's peace and hope in seemingly tragic and unfair circumstances. I believe He hurts when we hurt. I believe He holds us. I believe that His servants, like Mom and Dad who had been so faithful, are never promised safety. I believe we are not assured that everything will always go well. But, I believe we are held. The good news is that God came near, not that life will always go our way.

I believe He loves us. And His loving hands reach to hold us. When they do, I am reminded. When I sense His closeness, I am reminded of His scars. I am reminded that He knows how tragic and unfair the circumstances of this world can be. The death and injustice unfurled by the self-centered choice in the Garden became the tragic and unfair consequence that, through His hands and feet, was nailed to a tree.

Because He loves us. And, because His love is so mysteriously, thoughtfully, purposefully, steadfastly near, there is resolve. The same resolve that allowed Him to "set His face resolutely toward Jerusalem."

I saw it in Dad's eyes when he was learning to walk again. I saw it in Mom's eyes when I told her that she was a miracle and we were going to make it through this. I saw it in Erik, my brother, as we walked through that difficult season together. I heard it in my wife's voice when, with her nurse's heart, she spoke with passion about caring for Mom if she returned to Orlando.

It was that God-assured resolve that got us through that season. It was the fact that God is with us that reassured the resolve. And maybe that's why Jesus said that so much, "Fear not. I am with you." Because He never promised that we'd be OK. Just that we wouldn't be alone.

[a follow-up]

Mom died August 3, 2009, at 4:20 p.m. I was there. She had been trending amazingly well just two short weeks earlier. In two days, she spiraled downward and was gone. Mom did not want to be revived with those shock paddles if it ever came to that. I was the one who was there to tell the doctors not to do it. To let her go. And she did.

We miss her. So much. As Steven Curtis Chapman sang, "We will grieve with hope." We know that Mom's going doesn't mean she is gone forever. In fact, she is in forever. And we are still in time.

While here, our hope holds us up to remain steadfast in the love and on the mission we were made for. To live sent. And neither snow, nor rain, nor heat, nor gloom of night will stay us from the swift completion of our appointed rounds.

[CONSIDER and CONVERSE]

[1] How is God not safe? What are some specific examples from Scripture?

[2] What do you think about the prosperity gospel commonly preached in certain facets of American church culture? In your opinion, is it harmful? In your opinion, is it the truth?

[3] How does looking at the life and death of Christ clearly communicate that God does not play it safe?

[4] After reading the author's testimony of his mom's death, discuss what God is speaking to you about in this story.

[5] Where might Christ be calling you to live sent regardless of "the snow, rain, heat, or gloom of night"? Listen to Him and do what He says.

neither snow, nor rain, nor heat, nor gloom of night...

12

am I actually living sent?

(ten litmus test questions to help you discern whether you are or not)

[a story_Becky]

*B*ecky uses Craigslist. As a mother of three kids and wife of a high school basketball coach, watching how they spend their money helps them stretch their dollars. She stretches them really well.

Once she was looking for a particular item for their family and found that another mom who lived nearby was selling that exact item. She contacted her. They set up a safe place to meet. Becky exchanged money for the item, and she and the other mom talked a bit. They connected. Then, they left.

Becky felt a prompting to email the other mom to encourage her. She had recently moved to the area. When the other mom responded, Becky found out that she and her kids were looking for a playgroup. Becky told her about the one she goes to one morning a week and invited her. She came. She even brought a friend.

Becky is able to share love and life with her in a growing friendship. They are getting to know each other through playgroup all because they connected through the Web.

Living sent online through Craigslist can be a lot of fun. Ask Becky.

[ten definitive questions]

I have not met a follower of Jesus yet who, when asked to define church, does so as a place or an event. Everyone has said that the church is people. Why is it then that how those in church culture talk about, strategize about, and set goals for church communicates something different altogether? Why doesn't our verbal expression of a personal philosophy about church match our practical expression in the daily?

It is a fact that for many in church culture, the bridge from philosophy to practice is wide and gapped. So isn't it a fair question to ask—Am I actually living sent?

Sometimes believing something doesn't necessarily mean you act on it. I believe, for instance, that skydiving is exciting and relatively safe. But I ain't doing it. I do believe that the ways of Jesus are worth diving into. I realize more and more that His mission is not safe. I desire with all my heart for His ways to be my ways. However, I confess that I don't always take the plunge when He says it's time to move. Therefore, it would be fair to ask the following question. Am I actually fully engaging in the mission Jesus intended for His followers?

You probably agree that you should be living sent. You probably would not have read this far if you didn't. But are you? In order to help you discern whether you are actually bridging that gap between what you say you believe and how you are actually living, in order to decide whether you are actually being the church or just going to church, in order to determine whether you are actually living sent or, as my friend Charlie says, "living sat," here are ten litmus test questions to consider.

[1]   When you speak of church, what prepositions do you use?

We have already processed why this is an important question and not just a trivial matter of semantics. It's worth repeating, though. If you are mindful of how you speak of the church, which should certainly matter to you if you follow Jesus, then you will be mindful and intentional in how you live as the church. If you are intentional in the way you verbalize living sent, you will be more thoughtful and responsive to actually live sent as the church in your various spheres of influence. Jesus was very intentional in how He spoke of and prepared for the sending of His people, His church, and we should be too. So don't use to and from and in and at when you speak of church. Or any other words that refer to church as a place or event. The New Testament doesn't. Why should we?

[2]   When you think of missions, do you think of a missions trip to a distant city and a service project in your own community, or do you think about daily life among your family, neighbors, and co-workers?

Hopefully the answer is both. However, if when you think of missions you only think of the first half of the question, then I would suggest that you are not living sent. Rather, you are just doing missions. You are not living as a missionary, as a letter from God into culture. In the same way, if you are never engaging beyond your everyday encounters, I would suggest that you are not engaging fully as a missionary the way Jesus intended.

Read Matthew 28:18–20 and Acts 1:8 and emphasize them. But read Matthew 9 and 10 and emphasize them too. Jesus loves neighbor and nations, and sends us to both. Ultimately, He intends for His church to love every single person we encounter as though a neighbor and give generously into their lives no matter their background.

> [3] What is your common declaration about lost people around you? "Can you believe the way those people act?" OR "When can you come over for dinner?"

A friend of mine told me that one of his mentors once challenged him with this statement: "If those who follow Jesus would open their homes and their dinner tables to the stranger, then we'd eat our way into the kingdom of God."

What might happen if we actually opened up our lives and homes to the lost rather than just attempted to get them to church? I wonder if the reason American culture seems so disconnected from the ways of God is because the people of God are so disconnected from current American culture? More specifically, I wonder if they grow tired of feeling like we are trying to sell them something rather than loving them into the kingdom? Kindness leads to repentance, right (Romans 2)?

If you commonly comment about how the lost act, then you may have two issues to grapple with. One is your understanding of lostness. The other is your willingness to befriend people who aren't like you but are very much like those who loved being around Jesus.

We must understand that the way Jesus taught about the lost throughout Matthew, Mark, Luke, and John indicates that He simply considered them to be people who had not found their way yet or were simply so consumed with themselves that they couldn't see the way beyond themselves.

Think logically here. Don't even bring the Bible into this equation for a moment. A lost person is going to act lost. Don't be surprised when he or she does. And don't be arrogant when he or she does either. How easily we forget the weight of "there but for the grace of God go I." And how easily we forget that Jesus commanded us to love our neighbor. In fact, the most emphatic story He told related to that command included the challenge to love someone who was not only different but was even despised (Luke 10:25–37).

On top of that, who liked to hang around Jesus? And with whom was He most associated? Check out Matthew 9:9–13 (NASB):

> *As Jesus went on from there, He saw a man called Matthew, sitting in the tax collector's booth; and He said to him, "Follow Me!" And he got up and followed Him. Then it happened that as Jesus was reclining at the table in the house, behold, many tax collectors and sinners came and were dining with Jesus and His disciples. When the Pharisees saw this, they said to His disciples, "Why is your Teacher eating with the tax collectors and sinners?" But when Jesus heard this, He said, "It is not those who are healthy who need a physician, but those who are sick. But go and learn what this means: 'I desire compassion, and not sacrifice,' for I did not come to call the righteous, but sinners."*

Who likes to hang around with you? Fact is, people don't particularly like to hang around with people who condemn them more than offer hope to them. Jesus loved people.

What does that really mean? I would suggest this simple, but biblical, definition of love—to care more about what someone else is becoming than you do about what you are becoming. No wonder those tax collectors and sinners wanted to be around Jesus. Everyone else treated them like they didn't matter. He treated them like they did matter, like they were valuable, even worth dying for.

[4]   Is my tendency to disengage from culture and retreat into safer, more Christian environments, or is it to engage culture even amidst discomfort and danger?

Following Jesus is not safe. The current trend of Christians in America to try to create environments that shelter them and their kids from our culture, including the efforts to boycott certain organizations and to legislate righteousness, are not only self-serving but are also destructive to the mission of the church. Don't get me wrong. I'm not taking my six-year-old daughter prancing down Bourbon Street at 11:00 P.M. to help me hand out bottles of water and hangover pills taped to tracts. Common sense tells me better. But I am trying to raise my kids to know that being holy is not the same as staying clean from the world.

If that was the case, then we'd all have no hope. A holy God put on skin, became human, walked among the sinfulness of this world, and gave His own life to restore what we put in disrepair. He didn't stay sheltered and clean carrying that out. I would contend that the church is not actually following Him if we do not love like He loved and are not willing to be Emmanuel (among them), as well.

The psalmist does not describe God as a safe haven. Rather, He is described as a refuge and shelter. The word refuge alone implies a rest from difficulty and danger. The word shelter implies the presence of a storm. Those don't sound easy and safe.

If you spend more time at a family life center than you do at the local public gym, then you may not be living sent. If you participate only in church league recreational activities rather than the city league, then you may not be living sent. If you are constantly thinking about how to create a Christian moms' playgroup rather than participating in community playgroups, then you may not be living sent.

Why?

Are we scared? I was told recently that the number one command in the Scriptures is "Fear not." It's like Jesus knew we would struggle with the fear to engage. A friend reminded me recently of the story of John G. Paton, a courageous missionary surrendered to take the love of Jesus to the Pacific Islands during the 1800s, where it was feared that the inhabitants were cannibals. The captain of his transport ship questioned him, "You do know that you and your men will likely die if I leave you on this island?" The missionary replied without hesitation, "Sir, we died before we came here." Lord, please give me that kind of trust and surrender and courage.

Are we concerned about the benefit potential or damage potential?

In other words, are we so self-serving spiritually that we believe engaging culture will be of no benefit to the self-improvement track we are on? Or are we so self-preserving spiritually that we fear being pulled down spiritually unless we retreat to safety for development? I'm not trying to be ugly here. Just forthright. The mission Jesus intended for His church is vital and it is urgent! Being consumed with the comforts of the typical pursuits of the American Dream, as David Platt has challenged in his book, *Radical*, is not what Jesus intended. Platt declared in one of his teachings on that significance of this mission, "Church, we are plan A, and there is no plan B!"

Lord, help us to engage. Together so that we can hold each other up. Trusting You so that we can love without fear.

[5] When you hear "make disciples," do you think of a classroom or your relationships?

Without going back into all that we examined in the chapter on discipling, let's simply be reminded that learning and living the ways of Jesus goes far beyond the setting of a classroom. If you are attempting to be faithful to the mandate for every Christ follower to be making disciples of Jesus, but you only think of it in terms of enrolling people who are already Christian in a let's-go-deeper class, then you may not be living sent. There's nothing wrong with a great study together. However, discipling happens before someone even professes their faith in Christ and discipling continues far beyond the walls of a classroom into the halls of daily life. The classroom is simply one component of a discipling strategy. How are you being equipped and equipping others to disciple in the daily, not just the classroom?

[6] Do you spend a lot of time wondering whether you should quit your job to surrender to ministry, or do you simply live to minister to anyone and everyone where you are currently?

It is a common quote I hear, "I should quit my job so I can go to seminary and study the Bible and be a pastor. Then I could really do ministry!" Wait. Are you really thinking this through?

Now, I'm not in any way against seminary. I received my master's

am I actually living sent?

degree from seminary. Very meaningful experience that has had far-reaching implications into many facets of my life for years. Seminary is great.

And I'm not saying we don't need more leaders who dedicate themselves full time to equipping local expressions of the church. We do. We actually need more of them who are committed to learning with and walking alongside a local church for more than 18 months, far beyond the difficult season following the honeymoon.

And I am certainly not saying there's anything wrong with studying the Bible. What am I saying then? I am simply saying that if you have a job in the mainstream of the marketplace, then you have a ministry that most "pastors" will never have! And the only reason you should ever leave that ministry is if you sense a leading from the Lord to be a pastor/equipper, go to seminary, and serve full time with a local church family.

Think about it. Not only do people look at me funny when I say I'm on a pastoral leadership team, but often it also creates a wall between me and that potential friendship. That's just the way it is. But if you are a teacher, a CFO, a factory worker, a manager, a barista, an IT guy, a garbage man, etc., then you have an opportunity to share the love of Jesus in the normal rhythms of your life that most full-time paid pastors will never have. Why would you want to leave that vital ministry for the pastorate? Seminary is great, but it's not that fun. Get an MBA for crying out loud. It's marketable and there are more lost people in that setting to love and listen to and serve than there are in seminary.

[7] When you think of a friend who needs help, do you think, I need to get him to see the pastor OR I wonder what I can do to help?

The game that the church is fiercely involved in during the week is the real story of the church alive in a city, and the pastor/equipper is not the head coach as much as the water boy. I'm not saying they don't provide leadership. I'm just saying pastors should act less like Bear Bryant or Nick Saban and serve more like the equipment guys.

Maybe if this happened, then those in the game every day in the marketplace and in neighborhoods and among families would grow in the confidence to actually let the Spirit speak through them to someone rather than figuring out how to get them to talk to the professional wise-guy known as "pastor."

You matter. Your ministry is valid. If you follow Jesus, then the Holy Spirit resides in you. Listen to Him and say what He says when you are in situations where counsel is being sought. It is part of how you are walking in a discipling relationship with someone. Don't let the pastor/equipper have all the fun. You can thank me later. It's a great experience vital to living sent. And it's awesome to be a part of the Spirit using you to transform someone else.

[8]   When you think of heaven, do you think "kingdom come" or "kingdom is here"?

Wait before you answer. Even put this book down and go reread the Book of Matthew. Jesus clearly proclaimed that the kingdom was near, here even. "On earth as it is in heaven." The purpose of living sent isn't just to proclaim "pie in the sky by and by." It is to give people a taste of the God who came near. Jesus anticipated that as we love one another the way He loved us, that we would experience the kingdom now, not just when we die. So proclaim the heaven of the now that should exist among those who are living sent together—it is only a glimpse of what is to come. May we cultivate "on earth as it in heaven." If we are not, then we are likely not living sent.

[9]   Do you think godliness is measured with a mirror or within community?

Think on this one a bit too. This is a much bigger deal than it seems at first glance. If you are measuring how godly you are through introspection (evaluation with a mirror) only, then you may not be living sent.

John recorded a new command in John 13:34–35. Jesus told His followers they were to love one another as He had loved them, and that people watching them would know that they are learning and living His ways by their love for one another. It is a safe conclusion, then, that without love for one another in transparent, united, missions-centered community, we cannot live sent as letters of God's love and hope. Without love within a community of believers, people will not see us living as disciples of Jesus.

Furthermore, John also wrote in his first letter (1 John 3:14–19) the following, shared from *The Message*, because I think Eugene Peterson, the version's creator, translates this passage very practically:

The way we know we've been transferred from death to life is that we love our brothers and sisters. Anyone who doesn't love is as good as dead. Anyone who hates a brother or sister is a murderer, and you know very well that eternal life and murder don't go together. This is how we've come to understand and experience love: Christ sacrificed his life for us. This is why we ought to live sacrificially for our fellow believers, and not just be out for ourselves. If you see some brother or sister in need and have the means to do something about it but turn a cold shoulder and do nothing, what happens to God's love? It disappears. And you made it disappear. My dear children, let's not just talk about love; let's practice real love. This is the only way we'll know we're living truly, living in God's reality.

Did you see it? What John in essence is saying is that an intimate, shared life with God is most clearly demonstrated in intimate, shared life with one another. You show that you are godly when you live and love like God, not when you live and act like you have it all together.

If you are looking in the mirror for the measurement of your godliness rather than allowing it to be seen among your friendships, then you are likely not living sent. In fact, you are likely so self-absorbed attempting to live perfectly that you are missing out on His invitation to experience and give His perfect love as you live sent daily.

[10] Do you have a lost friend who would actually introduce you as his or her friend?

This is probably the toughest and most telling question among the ten. If you do not have a genuine friendship with a lost person, then you are not living sent. How could you be?

Now, I'm not saying that we don't need to live sent as letters of love to one another as followers of Jesus. John 13:34–35 declares it as a command to do so. However, it also provides the reason for why this command is given. So that everyone around us can see and know this Jesus we follow evidenced by our love for one another.

And, remember what Matthew 9 showed us. Jesus befriended the "tax collector and sinner." The One who was sent that now sends us (John 20:21) had genuine friendship with the lost or "those in need" as He called them. If we are to live sent the way the sent One intended, then we must have genuine friendship with the lost too.

I wonder if we too often approach friendship in terms of looking for friends rather than being a friend. We are loved, and as a follower of Jesus in particular, our "belief" in Him includes a trust that He so loved the world (John 3:16). We need to quit living to be validated by our friendships. We are loved! John in 1 John 3 declares that God has lavished His love upon us and calls us His children. Watermark sings it so well: "He goes before you now with a big, bright banner across this town saying 'Here comes my child! Here comes my child!'" We must begin living as already validated by the love of God and live sent with the intention to give that love away. Why? So that others can know and live like they are loved, too, as they walk in relationship with the God who is love (1 John 4).

Be honest. Do you have a genuine friendship with a lost person? If you don't, then you are not living sent.

Hopefully these ten questions have helped you discern whether you think living sent is a must and whether you are actually doing it. May we not just believe it, but act on it.

[CONSIDER and CONVERSE]

Go back and consider each of the ten questions. Pray through each one asking God for clarity on the ways you are not living sent and wisdom in the areas where a change of thinking may be required.

Also, consider walking through these ten questions with the followers of Jesus with whom you do life. Give honest evaluation then make an intentional action plan to surrender and be changed in any areas of concern.

13

live sent now

(four behaviors of cultivation seen
in those living sent)

[a story_Jen]

*J*en has five kids and wants more. Those five kids range in age from nine to newborn . People declare to her a lot that she has her hands full. In a very encouraging, unassuming way, she typically responds, "My heart is full too." She walks with her children daily with an unspeakable joy. Not that she doesn't deal with the common frustrations and all-too-common fatigue of a young mother, but she gets up in the morning and goes to bed at night thinking about the mission of loving her kids. She wants more than anything for them to see her listening to God and loving people. She hopes they will catch that and live by faith and in love too. That would be the greatest blessing to her heart. She lives sent to her kids.

And she encourages them to live sent to their friends. She holds them accountable to loving others, thinking of others before self. She battles self-centeredness among the siblings with tender fierceness, much like a gracious mother would.

Her husband is an interesting guy. Driven. Silly. Focused. Busy. Not all that handsome for such a beautiful wife (inside and out). He way overmarried. Jen is a woman like no other. She not only loves her kids, but she is a supportive, compassionate, patient, encouraging, loving wife who lives sent to her husband, as well.

He will tell you about her selflessness. He will tell you about how she lets him know that he is her man. How she cultivates his confidence and encourages him to dream. He will tell you how his heart wells up when he sees her pull one of the kids close and give them this face-to-face look that declares her unconditional love and everlasting commitment to her children. He will tell you of her contagious smile that melts his heart and makes him say yes to any request. He will tell you how she never abuses that power, but gently (and subtly) makes plans and moves forward in decisions together with him.

Jen lives sent to her kids. She lives sent to her husband. And he is grateful. And that he is me. Jen is my wife. I love you, Jen, more than I can say.

[cultivation]

Why do you think we have such a tendency to look for the how-to formula and the magic bullet for every action that we value? It's strange to me. Most certainly it is a product of the skin we wear wanting to be appeased quickly and the impatience with which we live. Neil Cole is someone I admire that understands the patience it takes to sow the gospel and live out the mission Jesus intended for us.

Neil is a cultivator. At least that's what I call him. He is the voice of a team of cultivators who work with church multiplication associates. They don't "plant churches," which I happen to affirm. They instead plant the gospel and let God blossom His church. And they've done it a lot. They've seen much multiplication.

One time, Neil shared with me a video of a story that I had read my children many times. It is from the classic "Frog and Toad" collection of children's stories. Frog has a garden. Toad wants one. Frog shares with Toad what he must do to plant a garden. What Toad must not have seen was what it took for Frog to plant a garden and then wait to see the growth that rises, because Toad plants his garden with some pretty high expectations. The next day he walks outside to his garden anticipating produce. When there is still only dirt, he becomes frustrated. Long story short, after much yelling at his seeds to grow, Frog challenges Toad that patience is an essential for cultivating. There are other essentials, as you would expect. Watering and sunshine and fertilizer and more. But patience may be the most fundamental essential of all.

Especially when it comes to the ways of the kingdom of God and what it takes to live sent daily. Sowing the seeds of the gospel of Jesus takes time. It is very much like the cultivation of a garden. The fruit that may one day come must not be manipulated, or it won't be as tasty as it might otherwise be. The produce must not be hurried or what is produced may not be true to the original.

It is epidemic in American church culture. Results now. Life change now. The gospel packaged and polished and understood now. But it doesn't work that way. It must not. Or God wouldn't have put the strategy in place before He even put time in place, He wouldn't have been so patient to plant a people in a land from which the Messiah would blossom at just the right time (Galatians 4:4), and He sure wouldn't have chosen to focus His entire movement mentoring ministry in the lives of so few people. He clearly understood that living sent is not a results-now kind of thing.

[live sent now]

So, why is this chapter entitled "live sent now"?

Well, we were five years into the cultivating of the gospel in a new community just north of Disney World and five years into emphasizing the importance of living sent and five years into watching God blossom this new local expression of the church when we sat back as a leadership team and asked an evaluation question.

Those people who were living sent, what had they been cultivating patiently that produced evidence that they had actually been living sent?

The evidence we were looking for was that of stories of lives changed by Jesus from people now living sent themselves. In other words, what were some common actions among those people who clearly were living sent? We discovered four. And we are quick to declare to you that these are not the magic bullet. They are not four how-tos to get live sent results now. Rather, they are four common behaviors of cultivation that you and I can adopt if we want to begin cultivating the gospel in our relationships daily and begin to live sent now.

[1. PRAY]

Now, don't close the book and storm off and grumble, "He did not just pull out the pray card as the cliché secret to effective evangelism. Oh no, he didn't!" Maybe you wouldn't say that, but you get the idea. Before you do whatever you might do when you read that one of the common behaviors of cultivation for living sent was to pray, read me out.

The common behavior that we noticed was not people living sent praying for a neighbor and a co-worker to know Jesus or be changed. While those are noble prayers, that was not what we noticed. No, the common behavior was not praying for "them" to be changed. Rather, it was praying that God would change "me."

I want to challenge you that if you want to live sent now, begin to pray for one neighbor and one co-worker. But here's the catch. Don't pray for them to change. Beg God to give you wisdom as to how you can love them exactly the way that they need to know love right now. Ask Him to continue to move you from a self life to a sent life and to open your eyes and heart to the specific way that you can simply love your neighbor and co-worker. Then, listen as you grow in friendship with them. You may be surprised. God is quick to answer prayers for wisdom, especially when linked to the mission He intended for His church rather than for self-serving purposes.

I've heard the stories. The book on love and insecurity that was given as a gift, and the response back that affirmed the deep need for such a book. The suggestion to grab some wings and watch the game, and the response back that affirmed the longing for more "guy time." The idea boldly shared to take the time to learn more about marriage, and the response back with tears of how badly her marriage is hurting right now. The note of encouragement sent, and the response back that it came on a day when he felt like no one cared. The Holy Spirit reveals the heart and life of someone before you have even had the chance to converse about it, and the neighbor or co-worker wonder if you have somehow bugged her cell phone or hacked into his email. How could you know?

Because you were cultivating the love of Jesus in their life by simply praying for God to change you to know how to love your neighbor or co-worker in some specific way.

[2. CONNECT]

*A*nother behavior of cultivation we noticed in those living sent was connecting in real life. Here's where your understanding of the church as a who rather than a what comes back into full view. If you think of church as a what, then you too often think of connecting with a lost person only in terms of inviting them to church. If you think of church as a who, however, then you think of connecting with a lost person in terms of them experiencing the love and beauty of the bride of Christ in the course of daily life with you and other followers of Jesus with whom you are friends.

No offense to anyone, but I have yet to meet a lost person who wants to add an event to his or her Sunday morning schedule. It is not to say that those who were lost but are now found will not want to make a priority of gathering to worship on Sundays or some other time during the week. It is simply to say that the chances of getting a neighbor or co-worker to the point where they might go with you to a worship gathering increase dramatically after they have done some real life with you. I'm talking normal stuff here. Eating together. Working out together. Watching the game together. Shopping together. Concerts and other cultural, community events together. Even serving together. Connecting in real, everyday life.

Several recent research studies were released on this very topic (one most notably entitled "Ten Surprises About the Unchurched" from www. BuildingChurchLeaders.com). All of them claimed that more than 80 percent of those considered unchurched would go to church with a Christian friend if they would only ask. It came out with that study that approximately only 2 percent of Christians ever ask. Wow! Eighty percent! The key finding in this study, in my opinion, isn't that the unchurched were interested in going to church. Rather, the key finding is that they would if a friend asked. A friend is someone they know who does life with them and connects with them on other occasions besides when they drop by to invite them to church.

Connecting in real life, in the normal course of your day, through the normal rhythms of your life is imperative if you want to live sent. Here are three suggestions as to why this is so important.

First, it forces those who say they follow Jesus and want to live sent to actually have lost friends. Believe it or not, that is a prerequisite to living sent. Now, you might say, "I have lost friends. I invite them to church all the time." But we are not talking about having friends who think of you as the annoying church friend. We are talking about friends who actually think of you when they have something to celebrate or to mourn. When they are ready to party or when they are in deep crisis. They know you as a friend who has their back, not as a friend who seems to be kind to them to help grow a church. This may be hard for some who call themselves Christians whose every relationship is rooted in some church event or organization. Jesus had lost friends who considered Him a friend. So should we.

Next, if we are truly going to live sent, then we must recapture the nature of evangelism as a compelling story to tell. "The Missional Church…simple" is a two-minute video that has spread via the Internet (you can easily find it on YouTube.com). It stated this concept very well: "Evangelism became equated with invitation." Telling the good news of Jesus is all about getting someone to the next great event, right? Wrong.

Jesus intended for His church to do more than invite someone to church. That is not a compelling enough reason for Him to die, and it's not a compelling enough reason for someone to consider the level of life change that would come if they followed Jesus rather than themselves. What is compelling, however, is the invitation to deny self and take up a beyond-self mission with far-beyond-me impact and follow the living Creator of the universe. That's a much more compelling invitation, don't you think?

Finally, another reason to connect with the lost over real life as we live sent daily is because they need to see the teachings of Jesus alive in our every day, not just on our Sunday. We keep finding that following Jesus begins to make sense to the lost when they see the ways of Jesus lived out in the daily rhythms of the lives of those living sent. Following Jesus is not a compartmentalized deal. His ways, alive in the ebb and flow of our living, make it even more compelling to a lost person to examine this Jesus we follow. If they only see Him in the polished productions of Sunday mornings, then they will not see how near Emmanuel has actually come and actually desires to come.

The issue here is not with those who are lost. The issue in this regard is with those who claim to be found. Jesus rebuked the teachers of His day who only taught the need to live for God. He contended that this kind of thinking leads to weary, religious effort, not abundant relational spirituality (Matthew 11). What if Jesus doesn't necessarily want us to live for God as much as He wants us to live with God? Emmanuel, the God who came near, is both the essence and embodiment of what God wanted to communicate to the world through His living Word, Jesus. If we hope to communicate that same message to those with whom we connect in real life, then Jesus needs to be central and noticeable in the daily rhythms of our activities and relationships.

[3. SERVE]

Yet another behavior of cultivation that we noticed in those living sent was serving locally and globally with that neighbor or co-worker for whom they were praying and with whom they were connecting. It is beyond amazing the way a people can taste Christ while participating with someone out of whom His love is pouring. One of my favorite stories to tell of this form of cultivation in motion is of Catalina (the full story was shared at the beginning of chap. 1) who is like family now to my wife and me.

We had met Catalina at the bank where our church family holds our accounts. Fast forward about ten months, and she was invited to help us with a service project in the community. We needed an interpreter. She knew four languages. She interpreted and tasted Jesus big time. It is a significant part of her personal story with Jesus. And a great example of how meaningful it can be to serve together with those to whom we are living sent.

Now, I understand that some people cringe a bit when they think about the possibility of the lost serving in the name of Christ. But think about how arrogant it is to assume that only the found can serve effectively. While there may be some coaching that is needed, why not take the chance? When is there not coaching needed for those who say they follow Jesus too? And how better for those who are searching out the ways of Jesus to see them in action firsthand? God can use anyone anywhere. And how impactful might it be for someone who is lost to serve alongside those who follow Jesus and possibly watch someone discover the fullness of Christ, whether through hands serving or lips telling or someone's heart believing?

Besides, among those whom I know that are lost, they are more eager to serve than most people I know within church culture. They have not been tainted yet by the overwhelming consumerism of American church culture that sterilizes hearts eager to serve with intellectualism eager to elevate. We are too clean to serve. We may need to rethink our approach and see serving with the lost, not just serving them, as an effective means of cultivating the gospel within our existing relationships.

[4. LIVE AND LEARN TOGETHER]

If you read the chapter on discipling, then you know that I believe discipling is more than just making converts smarter. It is an ongoing journey that doesn't begin post-conversion. Rather, as we live sent, we are privileged to be a part of the journey of an individual. Sometimes we see them trust and follow Jesus. Other times we long to see the produce but have to remain steadfast to trust God with the growth in the garden of their heart. Either way, discipling that person for whom we are praying, with whom we are connecting, and whom we are serving alongside is the ultimate behavior of cultivation among those living sent.

Stated another way, if you will pray for a neighbor and co-worker, connect with them in real life, and serve alongside them, I believe that learning and living the ways of Jesus will be a natural part of your friendship. You will disciple them as you are going, learning and living His ways yourself as they begin to see the reality and beauty and power of Jesus in their own lives.

I always think of my brother in this regard. Soon-to-be doctors walking through residency in the same teaching hospital share a lot of the daily rhythms of life together. Erik did just that with two colleagues who, by their own declaration, were not into the Jesus thing. Two years into praying for them, connecting with them, and even serving with them, one of them became open to a particular method of learning and living the ways of Jesus. Normally, in church culture, this method is commonly equated with discipleship. Based on Erik's experience (and many others'), it is certainly an important component of discipling but not the only one. That method? Bible study. His two friends wanted to study the Scriptures together. It was a big time breakthrough considering their apathy toward anything Jesus prior to seeing Him alive in the daily rhythms of Erik's life. And so he walked with them through Romans. You can only imagine the impact.

This very significant opportunity to go deeper in learning and living the ways of Jesus together with them opened up because Erik had already been learning and living the ways of Jesus with them. They just didn't know that school was in session. As Erik prayed, connected, and served with them, they saw Jesus and His ways face-to-face.

That is the beauty of living sent now. And those are the four behaviors of cultivation among those who are living sent. Not a quick fix. Definitely requires patience. But the produce produced is "on earth as it is in heaven."

As stated in a previous chapter, working with soil means getting dirty. And sowing seed defined by more than just the next great event may mean enduring droughts. But Jesus didn't intend for us to make clean, event-driven disciples. So, our "now" (meaning our every day) needs to demonstrate a commitment to living sent daily like the One who has sent us. Steadfast and sure. Intentionally focused on who others are becoming more than what we are experiencing ourselves.

That's why this is not just another packaged evangelistic approach or proselytization effort. This isn't about joining a religion. It is about meeting the Maker of life in the midst of the everyday lives of those who follow Him. Letters of His love into the now around us.

Let's get to cultivating.

[CONSIDER and CONVERSE]

[1]   Consider praying specifically for one neighbor and one co-worker/classmate whom you know. Pray daily not only for them, but pray for God to give you wisdom on specific ways they need to be loved right now.

[2]   What are some ways that you could connect in real life with this neighbor and co-worker? What do they like to do? What do they dislike?

[3]   Are you serving in at least one way locally and globally? In order to invite a friend to serve alongside you, you must actually be willing to serve too. Make a plan to start serving together.

[4]   Other than Bible study, which is very important, what are some everyday ways you can be learning and living the ways of Jesus with this neighbor and with this co-worker?

[5] Surrender the outcome of what might happen as you live sent to this neighbor and co-worker. Whether they become a part of your church family or not does not matter as much as them following Jesus and living sent together with a local church family. Remember, this is not about church growth. It is about people becoming who God intended them to be and experiencing abundant life as He intended them to experience.

14

sincerely,

(a signature of sorts)

[one final story_Taylor]

One final story, for now. I began these stories with a woman named Catalina. I want to end them with a story about a young man to whom she lived sent. It is summed up in an email Catalina sent to my wife. I'll let you read her words instead of mine:

Hi, Jen!

I'm finally able to sit down and share my awesome news with you! OK, do you remember how I told you the day I hung out with you that I was looking for people to go with me to the Joyce Meyer conference? Well, the Lord was truly at work, unbeknownst to me. I had mentioned it to Becky, Beth, and Lindsey, and none of them could go with me. The night before the conference, I was sitting in Taylor and Adam's apartment talking with Beth on the phone. Beth told me that if I didn't find anyone to go with me, she would go, but she had a lot of work to get done. When I hung up with her, the answer was standing right in front of me.

"Taylor doesn't work on Thursday nights, he can go with you, Cat," I thought to myself. So I invited him. He accepted!!! Tay was the last person I expected to go with me, but God had something else in mind.

Here's a quick bit of background on Taylor. I met Taylor at the same time as Meghan and Adam. We started working at the same place at the same time. They were interns. We all got promoted around the same time. Taylor and Adam do the same thing as Meghan. About four months after Meghan and I became roommates, Taylor and Adam became roommates next door. You've met Adam. He's been to gathering with me a few times, and he came to the Fourth of July party this year at your house. He grew up in a "Christian home" and follows Jesus. Taylor on the other hand, while he has mentioned to me that his faith is important to him as is his family, admittedly has not been living like it's important to him. He's been looking for happiness in different places. I think it's neat how the Lord paired up two faithful Christ followers with roommates that weren't as passionate about their faith.

So, a couple of weeks ago, when Adam and I were at gathering, Jim talked about who we need to be discipling and praying for faithfully. Adam mentioned to me that day that he and I need to be praying for Taylor and Meghan. We have been doing so ever since.

Back to the Joyce Meyer seminar. So, at the very beginning, Joyce Meyer opened up by asking if there were any people there who had never trusted Jesus as their personal Savior, or if there were any people who had already trusted Him, but weren't living like they had. She asked those people to rise in their seats and repeat a prayer. I stood up to pray with a woman standing behind me who was trusting Christ that very night. When Taylor saw me stand up, he stood up. We all repeated Joyce's prayer. The rest of the conference was great. I loved the message, and Tay seemed to be enjoying himself.

Now, what happened after the seminar, that's the exciting part! We were stuck in traffic in the Amway Arena parking garage. While we sat in the car, I asked Tay if he had enjoyed it and what he had liked the best. He went over the highlights of what Joyce said, and he told me that something she had said really struck a chord. He then admitted to me that he was tired of living the way he had been living, and that he wanted to start living like he had a personal relationship with the Lord! He told me he meant it, and that from then on, he wanted me to start holding him accountable. He said he's been feeling the Lord tugging at his heart for a while now.

You can imagine how blown away I was! Since then, watching the transformation taking place before me has been one of the neatest experiences of my life. It's as if a veil has been lifted from his eyes. He is so "gungho" about his new found faith It is a delight and encouragement to watch

What a story of living sent. Catalina's living sent didn't stop with her. It continues now with Taylor as he lives sent. He wanted purpose and hope. He found it renewed in following Jesus, the One who was sent.

[learning from an atheist]

When Jesus taught, He used stories. It's not that we should only use stories when we teach the ways of Jesus. When I teach, I use various forms of communicating. However, I never underestimate the power of a story to bring home a point of communication to someone. That's what this chapter is about—stories.

Before we dive into those stories of people living sent, let me just ask you a question: How much would you have to hate someone to not share with them how they can find abundant life now and forever, if you knew how and had abundant life yourself?

If you need to read it again, go ahead. Not because it is so complex and profound, but because it is such a piercing question.

It is not original to me. I heard it from an atheist. That's right. An atheist on a YouTube.com video that someone sent me. It was a video blog post, about five minutes long, of a man named Penn Jillette, of the Penn and Teller magician duo who are well known as headliners in Las Vegas.

Anyway, Penn video-blogged some of his personal thoughts about a man who came up to him after a show to give him a Bible with a note in it. Penn wraps up his thoughts by asking the question above. He, as an atheist, even compliments the man who loved him enough to be a letter of God's love to him that very night. The man's kindness clearly touched Penn. You can watch the video by going to this Web address: http://www.youtube.com/watch?v=ZhG-tkQ_Q2w.

This story I just shared is, in terms of email and mail, an example of bulk mail or junk mail. Not because it was insignificant. Don't misread me here. It was very significant. It's not junk in the sense of junk that you don't like it or that it is no good anymore. It is simply like forwards you get through email or like bulk mail through snail mail that is sent out to a large group of people that the sender doesn't even know. It is like a cold call in sales. The man who spoke to Penn had no relationship with Penn, but he delivered a "message" to him anyway.

I would suggest that this is a valid way to live sent, when the Spirit prompts us to do so. Here's why. When we receive bulk mail, it comes from someone we don't know. The sender doesn't know us, and we don't know the sender. However, when we, as letters of God's love, live sent to someone we don't know, we may not know them, but the Sender does. God knows them. And for whatever reason, in that moment, His Spirit may have prompted us to stop and connect with and speak to them in a cold-call kind of way. That is a valid way to live sent.

However, in most situations, God's Spirit prompts us to befriend people first. "My name is Jason. What is your name?" is a much better greeting than, "Hello, my name is Jason. I don't care what your name is. I am going to tell you about Jesus anyway." That is not love at all. That is not the kind of cold call the Spirit would call us to, because it is not loving. And the fear people have that causes them to be less intentional about sharing the message of Jesus with other people is typically based in that kind of thinking, which is an exaggerated example.

The love of Jesus isn't something to be shared with people coldly or sporadically. The love of Jesus should spill over out of my life onto people at every moment. The letter should be open and available to be read at all times.

We must, therefore, listen to His Spirit prompting us in the everyday on how to live sent to our families, our neighbor, in the marketplace, in local and global community, and on the Web. We must listen for His nudges, telling us to love in this way, to listen at this time, to be quiet and just be there in this situation, and to speak these words when appropriate. We either love the people around us enough to give away the life that has been given to us, or we don't care much about that other person's life.

This is not about helping them make a religious choice. This is life or death. Now and forever. And Jesus' strategy for helping people, who don't know that God came near, to know that He came near and to know that God loves them unconditionally right where they are is this—for his letters (the people who have come to know Him) to love them right where they are. They will know Him and know we follow Him by our love for one another (John 13:34–35).

[so, what now?]

S ound too easy? It is. Living sent is not easy to do faithfully, but it's easier to start than you think. If you can actually trust that what's been written and is being written on your heart and in your life is worth reading, then you can do it. And it is, because God is writing it and thinks you are worth dying for. And if you can listen to the Spirit of God in your heart as you follow Jesus every day, then you can do it. Because He will prompt you in who to serve and when to connect and how to befriend and what to say. And, if you love the people around you in your daily, then you can do it. Remember—to love someone means that you are willing to do whatever it takes to help them take a step toward abundant life. If we love people, we must be more concerned about how their life is filled up because of the love we spill out with no regard for how they return that love.

If you can trust and listen and love like that, and if you really think that the message of God coming near and giving us His love and hope in Jesus is a message worth your life's declaration, then you can do it. You can live sent too.

My friend Jim, whom I love deeply and who has walked closely with me since college and now on our equipping team with Westpoint Church, asked this very insightful question regarding people committing to live sent:

The question may not be What do I need to do to live sent

every day? The question may be this—What do I need to stop doing so that I can live sent every day?

What do you hold more valuable? What takes up more of your energy? What captures your attention? What gets you excited more? What matters more than being the letter of God's love and hope to a people who desperately need the abundant life Jesus died to give? I pray that these stories of living sent have inspired and encouraged and challenged you to live sent. What's stopping you?

Hopefully in reading this book you have realized that Live Sent is not another program you can take and use to grow your church. The missionary Paul wrote in the New Testament that God grows His church. We only plant and water His love into lives. And that's the point. This isn't another program to grow your church. It's simply what you were intended to be. Generously. Every day. Delivering a message that you believed. Meant to love and befriend, regardless of whether or not the person you live sent to ends up being a part of your church family. This is how you were made to live.

Remember, you are a letter.

[inviting you to the ongoing conversation]

Well, there you go. Five ongoing how-tos. Let me know how they are working for you. Let me know your suggestions. Let me know your stories. Share them at www.LiveSent.com. Or email me at InvitingConversation@gmail.com.

In the meantime, let me encourage you to work hard and stick with it. Leading a culture of people to live sent is not as easy as simply trying to get a few more people to show up on Sunday mornings. But it's worth it. It's exponentially worth it. It's kingdom worth it.

Keep telling people that they are a letter. As Jesus was sent, now He sends us. Let's live sent together.

sincerely

[CONSIDER and CONVERSE]

Process each of these five approaches and evaluate whether your church family's leadership are involved in any of them. Consider how they might affect what you are doing as you seek to cultivate a culture of people living sent.

P.S. . . .

(a note to pastors and other church leaders)

post scriptum

[a story_Billy]

*B*illy and his wife cheer for the Oklahoma Sooners. The only problem, getting to the game is a bit tough. They usually watch them on cable TV. One particularly important game, though, at the end of the season, was not televised.

Billy writes:

Ellie (my wife) and I had been in Port St. Lucie for a month and had watched all the OU games on cable. The last game of the year was OU vs. Oklahoma State, which is a HUGE game for us. Our local cable provider wasn't showing it, and neither were many sports grills, except one. The last place on my list said they were showing it. We decked out in our OU gear and headed to the grill that night.

While we were watching it, an older man (around 60) walked by a couple times intrigued by our OU stuff. At halftime, he sat down to talk to us. We talked for a few minutes, and then he asked why we had moved to Port St. Lucie. I told him that we were there to help start some churches. He was PUMPED! He and his wife had moved to a town about twenty minutes from Port St. Lucie just three months earlier. He and his wife were followers of Jesus and were excited to see that we had moved to their area to start new churches. We really connected that night and began hanging out together.

> The couple took an immediate liking to our daughter and loved on her like she was their own grandchild. About a month later, they called and said that God had told them to give $5000 to our family. Less than a year later they committed to pay for the auditorium rental for our new gathering space for new local church family (about $2000 a month).
>
> This couple never "joined" our church family, but they have been friends, encouragers, grandparents to our children, and BIG TIME financial blessings. I hate to imagine the past three years if that OU/OSU game had been on cable. The moral of the story is to watch games where people are.

It's a way to live sent. And give someone else the chance to live sent to you.

[cultivating a culture for living sent]

Not all letters end in a "PS," but this one does. And I hope this "letter" I've sent to you in book form has truly accomplished its purpose. I pray that you have been encouraged to take a hard look at the very way you think of the purpose of your life. I pray that you have been challenged in the very way you think of the purpose and mission of the church. I pray that you have been inspired to live your daily life as a letter from God into culture. I pray that you will no longer just "go to church," but that you will "be the church." I pray that you will LIVE SENT.

The addition of this "PS" is very intentional. "PS" in English means "Post Script," and comes from a latin expression that designated an addendum to a letter. Usually the author would remember something they wanted to make sure to mention at the end, or they would intentionally conclude the letter with specific thoughts directed at some party. In my case here, the latter is true. I am intentionally concluding the book with a note to a specific party.

It is directed to readers who might be pastors or church leaders who give themselves away to encourage and release people to be the church every day. Go ahead and read it even if you are not a conventional pastor, just so you can encourage your pastor to read it, and so you can know what to expect from your pastor if your local church family is to be a people who live sent.

If you are a pastor or church leader who equips followers of Jesus to live sent daily, then I am excited that you are reading this. I am simply going to share with you some thoughts that our pastoral team has learned as we have attempted to be a team that let's the church go to live sent.

I want to suggest to you five important principles that we've learned to be crucial in order to embrace the cause of living sent and actually lead others to be a culture of people who live sent. There are certainly more than these principles to be learned, but these are the five that I would say are pretty important. They are in no certain order. There's no magical reason for the fact that there are five. So, here goes.

[the church was created to be decentralized.]

I am a pastor. So, let me speak frankly to pastors. We, generally speaking but it's nearly always true, have fragile egos. We are not unlike most people who want to feel valued and who want to see value in what we do. So, no wonder we, again generally speaking but it's nearly always true, expend so much energy creating some "thing" that we can measure, feel proud of, and get patted on the back for, that it's no wonder we centralize the church.

Admit it. Examine what you consider to be the most important thing your church family does. If it is the Sunday gathering or even "Sunday School" or "small groups," then it is very likely that you are centralizing the church. Here's why I say that.

If you measure whether what you are doing is working based upon the number of people who are gathering on Sundays, then you are giving the majority of your energy to centralizing the church. Remember, I am not opposed to gathering or even having large gatherings. Just because you have one doesn't mean you value it as the most important thing your church family does. However, you do value it as the ultimate expression of the church if you measure your success based on how many come.

Also, if your "pastoral team" is responsible for coming up with every single way that your church expresses love and service and ministry, then you are centralizing the church. You are dreaming dreams and inviting people to join your dream, rather than looking for the dreams of people and serving them to see them come to fruition. If the way your church expresses love and service and ministry is based upon the blossoming dreams and strengths and passions of the body of people as a whole, then you are decentralizing the church.

All metaphors break down, so don't take this one to the very end of its implications, but what if we thought of "pastors" as "gatorade givers" rather than "CEOs" or "managers?" What if the real story of the church is about what people who follow Jesus are doing every day of the week in every sphere of their lives, rather than what we and the pastors get them to do on Sunday mornings? If the everyday matters most, then we must be gatorade givers. We must resource and encourage and serve people living sent daily, providing for them whatever refreshment and equipment they need to keep living as a letter from God.

This is what Jesus did. Don't miss it. Most organizations that do "church planting" would have dropped Jesus' funding, due to sporadic attendance (from over 5,000 to 3 back to 1,000 back to 3) and lack of "membership growth" and baptisms after two years of His ministry. Maybe success for Him wasn't how many were gathered, but rather how many were sent. Furthermore, not just how many were sent, but how many were sent from the sentness of those who were sent and then how many were sent from the sentness of those who were sent from the ones who were originally sent. And so on. Make sents? I mean, make sense?

Jesus clearly intended His church to be decentralized. I mean, He gave the "keys to the Kingdom" and the whole operations of the mission to really uneducated, unprepared, unpopular men and women. Why? He knew that they were not so reliant upon their own knowledge and understanding that they would listen to His Spirit to coach them along the way, through failures and successes, through persecution and through acceptance, through whatever came their way. So He sent them to be making disciples as they were going in the everyday. As they were going, not gathering. And when they gathered, it was catalytic for their sending, for their leaving.

Are you decentralizing or centralizing the church? Do you gather to worship and celebrate, but in the end to send?

The second principle is similar to the first. Function matters more than form. Having the right function is much more significant than making sure you have the right form. I say this, because I have seen many pastors come home from how-to conferences and adopt a new form, expecting transformational results. The typical result is disaster or disappointment. Fitting an unhealthy, ineffective function with a really polished, nice-looking form won't make the unhealthy, ineffective function healthy and effective.

However, changing the function will.

I am not saying that form is bad. Let's take the human body for example. It is the most formed, organized, systematic organism that I know. Many systems work together to keep the "function" alive and moving. Without the form, the function would be a blob. The form serves the function. The function doesn't serve the form.

The function of the local church should be, and in my opinion is, summed up in this very simple statement–LISTEN TO GOD AND LOVE PEOPLE. What else would you add to that? What "functions" of the church don't fit into that simple, functional description? Wouldn't you be pleased as a pastor if everyone connected with the church family you serve were listening to God and loving people? Wouldn't that be enough? Couldn't God blossom whatever He wants to blossom from the seeds being planted and watered into lives by a people who earnestly listen to Him and love people like He loves them?

If this is the case, why do we expend so much energy managing forms rather than releasing people for this function? Remember the who versus what stuff about "church?" It actually serves as a good filter for the "to-do's" of your pastoral teams and the ministry strategies and programs that you make priority. Ask–is what we are discussing, does it move the "who" forward to be the church, or is it about managing a "what?" Does it help people live sent? If not, don't do it.

This question especially applies to "form" stuff (programs and events and the like). Remember, these things are not bad. Form serves function and at times is even necessary in order for function to happen. Eyes are needed to see, for example. But we don't see just because we have eyes. We see, because God wanted us to see. He wanted us to have that function.

The same is true with a church "program." If a program exists because it has existed and everybody does it and your aunt and Seminary professor said this program was the most important thing the church has ever done and any leader that eradicates this program is lost and dying and going to the very pits of hell, but it does not in any way decentralize people to live sent or equip them to live sent daily, then it is an unnecessary form. That is a form that is not serving function.

However, if "Sunday School" is the primary way you connect people and let them experience doing life together and teach them to live sent, and then you actually allow those involved to share the stories of how they are living sent outside of that "Sunday School" time, then that is a form that is serving function. It's not outdated. It's functional.

What gets some pastors in trouble is when they start messing with the sacred cow programs of the "church" they are pastoring. You know what I mean. Those programs that certain people of supposed power live to preserve. I am sorry, but that is idol worship. If someone is giving more allegiance to a program of the local church than they are to Jesus and His mission, then that is idol worship. If that program is not effective in sending the people of that local church to love others in the everyday, not influencing the church to become more and more outward in their concern and intentionality for local and global community, and people fight to preserve it, then they are more passionate about that program than they are about Jesus. That is idol worship.

Pastors – lead gently in that situation. Love those people who consider themselves to have supposed power. Walk with them. Listen to them. Make sure they declare that they are passionate about the disciple-making mission of Jesus. And if they are, then have the courage to share with them that you think the program they fight to preserve isn't helping the local church to live on that mission of Jesus. Ask them to help you come up with another idea, or to change the functionality of that program. This approach is a loving approach, a leading approach, rather than a "lording" approach, which is what some pastors do, especially when they return from a conference fired up. Change takes time. Love is patient.

However, if you just stand idly by, and give the same preservationist energy to that "form" that is hindering "function," then your idleness may be an indication that you have joined in on idol worship. Be careful.

I don't want to beat a dead horse here, so I will dismount. I hope you get the picture. If not, I will give you my email at the end of the book and you can email me. Not because I know everything. It's obvious I don't. But because I have found that the best way to learn and grow is in the midst of relational dialogue. Let's learn and grow together, so email me if you have any questions.

[be willing to release all-stars.]

Have you ever seen a pond or small lake that has no outlet? Over time, it becomes stagnant. It retains the same water. It starts getting green. The water has no movement. Pretty much everything in the water dies. It's pretty ugly.

My heart hurts, because I fear that I may be describing a lot of local churches. Stagnant rather than on movement. And just as it is clear that water was meant to move and have a purpose, so the church is meant to be on movement and on God's purposes.

Why do some expressions of the local church become stagnant? The answer I am about to suggest it not the only reason, I am sure, but I would suggest it is one of the reasons. I believe that churches get stagnant because they retain all-star leaders rather than release them. People who were intended to be moving and purposeful who instead are hindered in that movement, for whatever reason, become stagnant and frustrated and discouraged.

Side note–all metaphors break down. And this "all-star" metaphor certainly does. In my opinion, every person who follows Jesus is an all-star, or at least should be. Every person who is a part of a local church family is a "most valuable player" according to what Paul taught in 1 Corinthians 12, or at least should know that Jesus thinks that way of them. It is understood that certain people have more influence than others. However, everyone has influence, and everyone who follows Jesus should never underestimate the value of their influence.

Having said that side note, now, let's continue in the metaphor of all-stars. Why don't pastors release all-stars? I wonder if it is the same reason fans of sports teams cringe when the general manager releases or trades an all-star. Those fans do not think that all-star is replaceable. Those fans do not think that the team will be any good without the all-star. Those fans would probably say that the team cannot afford to release that all-star.

I would suggest that local churches cannot afford to NOT release all-stars. At least if they are serious about God's kingdom over their own. The reason we cannot afford NOT to release all-stars is this–the mission and movement Jesus began is now passed on to us. While we are in this game, if we don't release the all-stars and trust that God will raise up the next most valuable player to replace them, then we will not have the privilege of seeing God's kingdom blossom up around us elsewhere. Also, we cannot afford NOT to release all-stars, because our failure to release them ensures the failure of what we are ultimately called to as the local church–to make disciples.

Disciples are disciplers in their truest expression. This implies being sent. And the ones who become "learners" (disciples) will reflect what they have been taught by the discipler. If that discipler is retained rather than released, then those learning will learn retain instead of release, and the movement forward and outward shifts to inward and stagnant.

All-stars were meant to play. Not sit on the bench. Listen to this story.

I was up in Lexington, Kentucky, visiting with a guy named Kevin who runs Live Wire Coffee and Music in the neighboring town of Richmond, Kentucky. On the way back to the airport, we stopped for supper. Kevin invited his friend. Kevin's friend used to be the CEO of Lexmark. Before he even really knew my name, we sat down and he began to vent.

"I am sick and tired of pastors who don't see the value of the business leaders in their congregations. They focus them on being an usher, when they should be ushering them out the door to be living for Jesus and using their God-given abilities for kingdom purposes every day."

I smiled. I liked him immediately. I was even more thrilled when twenty minutes later (seriously–he went on a tirade) I was able to share with him that we are trying our best not to do that. I told him I would be more than grateful if we turned out hundreds of business leaders who lived sent every day. I would actually be disappointed if we turned out 100 conventional pastors but fewer pastors into the marketplace.

Why? Because I believe in releasing all-stars. Our local church expression will always be being rejuvenated and refocused if we are releasing all-stars and watching new ones emerge.

Yours will too.

[a missional church doesn't just do occasional "missions."]

*P*eople are saying that the word *missional* is an overused word. That may be the case, but I still think it is an appropriate word. The word *the* is overused, too, but it is still appropriate. So is the word *missional*.

Maybe *missional* as a word is new to you. If so, here are five really good resources available out there to give you some different perspectives of and helpful insight into what being *missional* is all about:

* *Unstoppable Force* by Erwin McManus
* *Breaking the Missional Code* by Ed Stetzer and David Putman
* *The Forgotten Ways* by Alan Hirsch
* *The Tangible Kingdom* by Hugh Halter and Matt Smay
* *Organic Church* by Neil Cole

Maybe you are so familiar with the word *missional* that I just turned you off so much that you gagged uncontrollably, threw the book down, and stepped outside to let out a visceral scream. If so, I hope you felt relieved. I also hope you came back to read the rest of the chapter.

I have been asked on several occasions if the phrase *live sent* is nothing more than another way to say *missional*. That may be the case, depending upon how you understand missional. What I am really trying to say with *live sent*–well, instead of trying to explain it here in this paragraph, let me recommend a book that at least attempts to explain it. It is titled: *Live Sent: You Are a Letter*. Wait, you are reading that book. Oh. Good.

What was I saying? Yeah–*live sent* certainly is and I think should be a part of the missional discussion happening and the missional challenge that has been issued. I am fine if you equate it with the word *missional* as long as you understand the word *missional* to be about the purpose and mission and intention of a follower of Jesus' daily life. I am not fine if you equate *live sent* with the word *missional* if you just understand *missional* as a seasonal or trendy focus for a local church family on local missions projects. We were made to live sent. We were made to be on mission daily. We were made to be letters of God's love. We were not made to just sign up for an occasional missions project.

Alan Hirsch I would suggest communicates it very well in one of his more commonly repeated statements: "A church is not missional until missions is no longer an add-on but rather central to the entire agenda of the church." In other words, living sent is what drives everything a local church expression does. It is not merely the "evangelistic emphasis" or the "church growth method" of the church. And it is expressed in more than an occasional service project or international missions trip.

All that said, let me say this (or write it). If you are reading this or any other book about being missional, and you only think about stressing the importance of "local missions" in your community, then you may not be thinking about *missional* in the way that those who emphasize being *missional* are thinking about being *missional*. Does that make sense?

I would suggest that a lot of the people in church culture who hear someone speak about being missional are hearing the speaker say one thing and are processing what has been said in an altogether different way. The speakers are usually challenging those listeners to focus on helping people understand how important it is for their local church family to see their everyday lives as on mission to love people like Jesus loved us, where every encounter with every person in their everyday matters. The listeners are too often taking away from that message the importance of going back to tell their local church family how important it is for them to be really loving their local community and being on mission there. As a result, instead of seeing the church as a people that need to be released for the everyday, they operate out of the thinking that scheduling more service projects will accomplish being missional.

I am suggesting this as the case, because I have seen it over and over again with church leaders that we know around Central Florida and beyond. It is great to serve the local community. I AM ALL FOR THAT!!! Our church family certainly tries to do that. But there is a difference in stressing the importance of signing up for a local missions service project and stressing the importance of people living as a letter of God's love to their family, their neighbor, in the marketplace, in local and global community, and on the web everyday.

The difference is that you don't have to sign up for the everyday. You don't add that to your schedule. It is your schedule. It is "as you go" as Jesus commanded in Matthew 28:18–20. You don't add it to your schedule for this coming Saturday and dress in paint-stained clothes. You simply BE THE CHURCH, be on mission, living sent every single day at every single moment to every single person you encounter. Loving them as Jesus loved them and how the Spirit prompts you to love them.

One side note. I am not knocking local or global mission projects here. I think they are great. I agree with one leader who recently wrote this in one of his twitters: "I think churches that are trying to be missional must not forget about missions." I agree. Mission projects and trips are often not only impactful for the communities that are served, but they are also life-changing and catalytic for the people who go to serve. I am all for them.

I just think that "missions" has been emphasized for so long over the importance of every follower of Jesus living sent in every day life, that church leaders fall back on it and say they are being "missional." Maybe that's because you can measure how many sign up and show up for a mission project. It's tougher to measure how many are living sent and how they are doing at living sent.

Like my dad has always said, "If it's worth doing, it's probably not easy." And emphasizing living sent is definitely worth doing. People need to read God's letter everyday. They'll read it in the lives of His followers. Their lives depend on it. So, we must stress people living sent everyday even more than we try to get them signed up for missions. But do that too. Just not every weekend.

[people only do what makes sense.]

You are probably saying, "Duh!" Well, hold up before you dismiss this principle as vital for leading a culture of people who live sent. This principle is actually transformational for leading in any setting.

I heard the statement for the first time from Harold Bullock (HaroldBullock.com). He pastors a local church expression called Hope

Community Church in Fort Worth, Texas. He has for a long time. He is a very wise leader for whom I have deep respect. He and the Hope Community church family have influenced and inspired and sent leaders out to start over 200 ministries around the world. That's really amazing.

Harold told me this over lunch back in 2003. A friend of mine knew my wife and I were about to embark on the adventure of trying to see a new church blossom in the midst of a new community on the west side of Orlando. That friend told me I needed to meet with Harold Bullock before I did. So, he flew me and flew with me up to see Harold. It was a very meaningful time.

Harold said many wise things in the conference we attended, and he said many very wise things over lunch with my friend and me. But none more transformational than this simple statement.

It's funny, but most leaders I know, whether they would admit it or not, lead out in a new task and completely expect people to follow them because of their sheer charisma and the excitement of the new task. The fact is, though, that most thinking, influential people will actually not follow because of sheer charisma and the excitement of the new task. They will only follow your lead and get excited about what you are suggesting WHEN IT MAKES SENSE TO THEM.

I don't really think I need to give examples to you, but let me give one just in case. People thought the world was flat. A lot of people. It made sense to them, because everything they saw and knew looked like it had a beginning and an end. This was the thinking about our great globe for quite some time. There were teachers and scientists and explorers who espoused other hypotheses, but they were not believed by most people, because the world being anything but flat did not make sense to them. So, those teachers and scientists and explorers had to make it make sense to them. This was no easy task. Many lost their lives in trying to prove that we lived on a big, rock ball. But they did. And everyone I know today believes that the world is round.

Almost everyone I know today still calls Sunday morning "church." Almost everyone I know today, even the ones who espouse "missional" ideas still emphasize "going to church" over "being the church." Almost everyone I know today still sees "church" as a "what" rather than a "who." Because it makes sense to them in their thinking and their vocabulary that

Post scriptum

church is Sunday morning, gone to, and is a thing in which you participate.

And yet, many of these same people assert that we should be living "missional lives." Why? Because it doesn't make enough sense yet to them to change their vocabulary and how they speak about "church" and what they stress about the strategic ministry of the church. People only do what makes sense to them, and it has not made sense yet.

The same is true of the people you are trying to convince to be a part of something you believe to be of utmost importance. It may be at home, at work, in your community, among your friends, with your local church family. Doesn't matter. This principle applies across the board. And if you and I will put serious energy into making something make sense to people, something that we know is of utmost importance, then those people are much more likely to join in.

This takes time. Lots of coffees and meals and meetings with people. Lots of hearing their perspective. Lots of them hearing yours. But if it really is of utmost importance, and you really focus on helping them see why this makes complete sense and why this is of utmost importance, they are much more likely to join in.

I know. Our team has spent the last five years stressing living sent to people who have a church background and to people who don't. And it has taken a lot of time and a lot of mistakes and a lot of coffees and a lot of meals and a lot of phone calls and a lot of emails and a lot of messages and a lot of teachings and a lot of a lot of other stuff. But today, while we are small in number, we have the most committed group of people who believe in the mission of living sent, and we have sent out so many, many people across the nation and even some across the globe who are committed to live sent in their new contexts.

All because people do what makes sense to them.

[bottom line_the key is security.]

Well, there's those five principles I mentioned. One more thing about those, before we move on to the "PPS" chapter with five specific "how-tos" on leading a culture of people who live sent.

There is an underlying question here, and the answer will affect whether you truly lead by these five principles in your attempt to lead a local church family to be committed to living sent as Jesus intended us to be. Here it is:

Are you secure enough to lead like this?

You have to be, or you will not lead like this. You will not decentralize. You will not focus on function over form. You will not release all-stars. You will not give priority to something you can't measure well. You will not be patient enough to relate to people and help living sent make sense to them.

However, if you actually believe that God loves you, then you might be secure enough. If you believe that, while a local church family may cut you a paycheck, you actually work for the living God, then you might be secure enough. If you actually trust that "whose you are" (you belong to God who has declared you worth dying for) is more important than "who you are" and "what you accomplish," then you may be secure enough. If you actually love people, which means you are more concerned about them becoming all that God intended them to be than you are about them all thinking you are a good leader, then you may be secure enough. If your hope is actually in Christ alone, not in the "church" you grow or don't grow, then you may be secure enough.

But you have to be secure as a follower and a leader in order to lead a culture of people to live sent daily.

I am not saying that you won't ever or don't ever struggle with insecurities. I am not saying that you don't have to battle the temptation of needing everyone to give you the credit instead of God the glory. I am not saying that there won't be days when you wonder if you are even doing the right thing and if this is going to work.

I am simply saying this—when all that happens and when all else fails, you know that you are not a failure. Because, in the words of John Lynch from Phoenix, "On my worst day, I am still John Lynch in Christ." On your worst, most scared, most doubtful day, you are still in Christ. You still belong to God, and He is still near to you.

Trusting in whose you are will help you to be secure enough to lead like this. And if you are secure enough, you may actually fulfill what Jesus said about His followers. He said that we would do even greater things than He did (John 14). You see, these five leadership principles I previously mentioned pretty much come from examining what Jesus did with His

post scriptum

immediate followers when He walked the earth. It worked pretty well. He started a movement that hasn't ended.

Be secure enough to join His movement, rather than thinking you've got to start your own.

[CONSIDER and CONVERSE]

[1] Do you feel like the local church family you are a part of has a culture for living sent? Why or why not?

[2] Based on the definition given of "missional," is your church family missional?

[3] Do leaders feel restrained or released among your church family?

[4] If you are a pastor/equipper among your church family, then what are some areas of insecurity for you? Are you communicating those and praying with anyone about them?

[5] If you are not a pastor/equipper, how are you supporting and encouraging those trying to equip you to live sent?

PPS...

(suggestions for pastors/equippers wanting to equip people to live sent)

[a story Erick and Mandy]

*E*rick and Mandy are living sent in Manhattan. Erick is a journalist with a profound heart to serve and a significant gift of teaching the Bible. He does each one whenever the chance is presented, and every now and then all three together. Mandy is a teacher. She lives sent to a classroom of middle schoolers and her colleagues on faculty at a high-needs school in west Harlem. She has a sincere love for people and a gift of discernment to see into their lives, see who they really are, and see what they really need.

Erick and Mandy have an apartment there in Manhattan. My wife and I stayed with them at their previous apartment. It was roughly 650 square feet and leased for $2,475 a month. What Manhattanites gain by riding the subway and not having a car, they lose in paying higher rent costs. Their new apartment is bigger, but even when it was small, they continuously lived sent through hospitality and genuine care. They had people over when they needed lodging. They had people over for meals. Doing more than having a residence. Actually giving away that which had been given to them (or better said that they paid enormous rent for).

Erick and Mandy are living sent in one of the most influential cities on earth. And, their light is shining. I am more than proud of them. I love them and how they are living letters from God everyday.

[five ongoing, intertwined, intentional, relational approaches]

I want to suggest five basic how-tos for leading a culture of people to live sent. One disclaimer. You have to be careful to not try to make discipling, into a linear process. Living sent is not an A to Z process. It is an ongoing deal. Jesus loved to use participles (–ing words) when He taught. He saw life as ongoing, His love as ongoing, His mission as ongoing. And He emphasized it in His language and in His form. We must, as well. In our forms, we must emphasize the ongoing element. This is not a linear process with a start and finish. It is never-ending. At least until Jesus returns.

So, these five how-tos are not intended to be a start and finish type of deal. They are not a linear process. They are not done in a particular order. They are always happening. They must always happen if you are going to lead a culture of people to be living sent.

Here they are, not numbered intentionally in order to emphasize that there is no specific order, and given as participles in order to emphasize their ongoing nature:

[shifting construct]

*P*eople think a certain way and see life in a certain way, because of the "construct" or "framework" or "paradigm" their thinking is based upon. I am going to assume in writing this section that you understand that and agree with that. Like the example I gave in the last chapter about the world being flat, people are going to hear everything you as a pastor are trying to say through their construct.

Here's what this means. No insult to your intelligence if you already know this, but it's simply a principle of communication. You have a speaker. You have a hearer. The speaker says something. Now there's a message in the air. The hearer hears it. The hearer processes the message. The hearer hears that message through the framework of the way they always process things. The hearer begins to understand that message based upon their preconceived notions. The hearer hears the message through the construct that has been constructed over the course of their life. The hearer, therefore, may or may not hear the message the speaker intended for them to hear, depending upon whether the speaker's construct and the hearer's construct are kindred. If they think about the topic of the message in similar fashion, then the message will be well communicated. If they do not, then the message may be heard, but what the speaker intended to communicate will not be heard by the hearer as it was intended.

What does all this mean?

Well, when it comes to "church," you can lead and communicate with very good intentions, but if you do not learn what the construct of your hearers are, then you will not be communicating very well. Why? Because every message you communicate will be filtered through the way the hearer thinks about "church." Unless your hearers and you have a similar way of thinking about "church," the message you intended for them to hear will not be heard. They will filter it through their construct, not yours.

So, as a leader who hopes to lead a culture of people to live sent, if you do not work at addressing the construct of those people, they will not hear the message you are trying to communicate. If they think of "church" as something they go to instead of who they are in the everyday, they will hear you teach about living sent, but they will not process it into their daily lives until their construct changes. Make sense?

Working hard at shifting constructs must be a premier "how-to" of your to-do list and your strategy if you hope to lead a culture of people to live sent. It is most assuredly an ongoing effort and a never-ending priority. If it is not, you will be saying one thing and your hearers will be hearing another, and together you will not live sent, as a result of that disconnection in communication. Or, they may hear you and do things that you do not see as living sent, since they are hearing and processing through different filters than you spoke from.

Here's the deal. To simplify it, I want to suggest you focus on two specific areas with regard to shifting a person's construct of "church."

First, stress that "church" is a "who" and not a "what." Stress that it does not happen on Sunday morning, but all throughout the week. Stress that the real story of the local church is not told on Sunday mornings, but as the people (the church) are living sent every day in their various spheres of life. Stress this in your language (you can't call Sunday morning "church" if you don't want them to think of it as "church"). Stress this in your messages. Stress this in your enewsletters. Stress this on your website. Stress this through your blogging. Stress this when you have coffee with someone. Stress it to your kids. Just stress it.

Second, stress that people make befriending other people a priority. Yes. I just wrote that. In case you haven't noticed, all of us like who we like and typically don't hang out with people who are different than us. So, in church culture, what this means is that those who call themselves "Christians" tend to only know other "Christians" and avoid those who are not. This is true in their neighborhoods and at work. We MUST operate on the principle that there is always room for one more friend in our circle of friends. We MUST be intentional to see the beauty of every person. We must be a friend, not just have friends. If you are not willing to have friends who are not followers of Jesus, then you are not willing to live sent. If you are not willing to cultivate friendship with whomever, then you are no different than the guy who asked Jesus about who he really had to be neighborly to. We MUST make befriending people a priority if we want to live sent.

Believe it or not, both of these require a lot of attention and effort in what you communicate and how you communicate. They are key elements of focus in shifting the constructs of people.

[inviting conversation]

*A*nother ongoing how-to that relates closely to shifting constructs (remember all of these go together rather than progressively) is that you must be inviting conversation. It amazes me how many pastors and leaders isolate themselves from the people they hope to serve and influence. How irrational is that? To think that we would be conduits for change in the lives of people we don't even interact with.

Not sure why this is. I really think it usually goes back to the security issue I mentioned in the last chapter. Are you secure enough to allow other people to speak their minds, to disagree with you, to tell you what makes sense to them? Are you secure enough to invite conversation?

I absolutely, firmly believe what I am about to write, and I have seen it work over and over again in many different spheres of leadership and life. The main way you will influence a culture of people to make a construct shift about the "church" and actually live sent daily is through inviting conversation.

You have to actually build a relationship with the people you are leading and have ongoing conversation with them. By ongoing conversation, I mean face-to-face over coffee or a meal. I mean through email. I mean over the phone. I mean via text messaging. I mean through Twitter and other social networking platforms. I mean in your writing and your teaching. Conversation can happen in many ways. It becomes ongoing when you are walking in relationship with someone who hears your message in all those forms and has access to talk with you and other leaders who are communicating living sent.

I would suggest that real transformation of construct happens in the midst of relational dialogue. A person's values and beliefs and philosophy and construct change first. Then, it is reflected in how that person lives. Then, their behavior is not just modified, it is transformed.

For this to happen, you have to make having relational dialogue with the people you lead a priority if you want to shift their constructs. It won't happen just through good teaching on Sunday morning.

If you want them to be living sent, you have to be inviting conversation. Did I mention that this takes time? It takes time. You probably ought to get to it.

[sending leaders]

A third ongoing how-to is sending leaders. This has to be an intentional part of your to-do list if you are going to lead a culture of people who live sent. Really, in the last chapter, we covered a significant portion of what this how-to is all about. Please feel free to go back and reread principle # 3 that I shared in the last chapter. To add to that, here are two suggestions.

One, pray for discernment to see every single person's area of leadership. No matter how big or how small, everyone leads in some way. Everyone has influence. Everyone leaves a wake, no matter how wide or how narrow it spreads. Pray for God to help you see the area of leadership for every person you lead, and then encourage them in that. Whatever it is. Wherever it is. Whether it helps what you are passionate about or not.

Two, pray for discernment from God's Spirit to notice catalytic leaders. Really, everyone leads in some way. What I am talking about here is the focus of looking for leaders who you notice are catalytic in the lives of many others. Look for influencers. Not just in what your local church family does together. Look for what they do in their families, communities, and at work. Notice who the people are that really touch and change lives. Then, walk with them.

This is not about showing favoritism. DO NOT DO THAT. Don't

hang out with someone cause they are a "big whig." Jesus isn't about that. You and I cannot be either.

I am talking about people who are influencers in various spheres of living, and it does not matter what their position or title is. If they are influencers, then come alongside them. If they already see how significant their influence can be in sharing the love and hope of Jesus, then keep encouraging and resourcing them in that. Especially to their family. However, if they don't see it yet. Converse with them in an ongoing way and help them to see it. When they see it, when it makes sense, then they will begin to live sent in all the ways in which they are catalytic influencers.

Then, don't be tempted to bottleneck them by burdening them with your agenda. If God wants them to fit into any dream you have, He will definitely make that clear. However, it is more likely that He may be blossoming a dream in their heart. Be willing to send them to follow God in that dream He is blossoming in them. Even if it means they move or go somewhere else. That's when it gets tough.

But sending leaders is why this movement Jesus started is still going. We must do it too.

[coaching contextually]

A fourth ongoing how-to is coaching contextually. We unpacked contextualism earlier, so I won't spend time unpacking it further here. But "coaching contextually" is actually a tool for you as a leader to be able to better lead people to understand their daily surroundings and live sent in their context. Here's how. By the way, I will admit that most of what I am about to write about coaching I learned from Jane Creswell, Margaret Slusher, Damian Gerke, and Bob Bumgarner.

Let me start by asking a question? Who's your favorite coach? If I told you mine was the old western stage coach, would your first reaction be, "Huh???" Well, it all depends on what is meant by the word "coach," right? If I am talking about a basketball coach, then that means one thing. If I am talking about a *coach* that carries people and is drawn by horses and takes you places, then that is another thing. Usually, we think of coaching in terms of athletic metaphors, not transportation. But what if we did?

I am not saying that the sports metaphor for a leadership coach is invalid. It certainly is valid, and there are many lessons to be learned from the best coaches who have ever coached in sports. Many of them not only knew their respective games, but they knew how to connect and motivate and unite players for both games and the game of life. There's much to learn from them.

For the sake of this how-to, though, at least to begin with, and since we are talking about living sent as we are going, let's see coaching as a vehicle. In the midst of those relational dialogues, those transformational conversations, view your questions and suggestions as vehicles for moving a person along toward a better understanding of and a better follow through on making disciples / living sent.

Instead of lecturing people to death, whether in front of a large group or over coffee, ask pertinent and focused questions that can help that person you are walking alongside see the need to live sent and the many opportunities they have to do so. It's strange how different a person treats an opportunity when they think it is their idea. And when your coaching is like a vehicle of discovery in an alongside manner rather than an I-have-all-the-answers manner, you will see people own what they discover. And, you may learn a thing or two along the way.

Another aspect of coaching contextually involves helping someone learn and trust their God-given value. Otherwise, they cannot be released to be the letter that Jesus intended them to be. If they are able to have coaching conversations with you that help them know their value, then they will be able to live confidently in Christ delivering His message. This conversation may include walking through issues about trust and distrust, about forgiveness and grace, about religious legalism and intimate relationship. It may involve in-depth looks at what humility and confidence and decentralization really are. Whatever the conversation turns toward, the bottom line is this – people are most hindered from living sent when they doubt whether they are worth reading as God's letter.

Another aspect of coaching contextually is actually having coaching conversations about the context in which the person you are coaching is living sent. They must be able to clearly see their context and get to know the people that live there. You can help the person see what's going on around them mostly by actually going to specific crowd spots in the context and asking pertinent questions. Instead of trying to unpack the whole deal here, let me encourage you to connect with Hal Haller about context. He, in my opinion, is the best at teaching and coaching people contextually. His website is http://www.churchstrategydesign.com.

Finally, let the goal of your coaching conversations be that the person you are coaching grows to have a deeper and deeper commitment to their mission, specifically smack dab in the middle of their context. Let me put it bluntly – some people like the glamour of being known as a minister and a leader and an influencer more than they do for actually loving the people in their context. Jesus saw the crowd and had compassion on them (Matthew 14). We tend to see the crowd and get annoyed. That's not a deeper commitment to our mission. It's evidence of selfless selfishness. That's what I call it when we want to act selflessly in order to be known as a selfless person. That's selfish. That's not commitment to the people of my context that Jesus loves and that I am called to love like He did.

We need to be coaching contextually with these emphases so that people are released to live sent in their contexts, and so that those people we have coached see coaching as easy enough that they can do it among the people that they lead and release.

[capturing stories]

A fifth ongoing how-to at first may seem unnecessary. However, let me challenge you to not underestimate the power of capturing stories of people living sent and sharing them in creative ways. Stories really make a difference in helping you to bring to real life a principle or point you are trying to get across.

Why is that? I guess because stories make the point of your message more real, like it could really happen. I guess because stories of people living sent in everyday life make the everyday person feel like they actually live sent, too. I guess because stories evoke emotions that connect people with the importance of living sent. If you can capture stories of living sent and share them well, you more than likely will inspire more people to live sent.

Here's what we've seen. This particular how-to works in tandem with the shifting constructs how-to, usually in a cause and effect kind of way. Here's what I mean. At times, we've captured and shared stories of people living sent and people have been inspired. They inquire more about it, wanting to connect with us and learn more what living sent is all about. When they do, we are able to enter into relational dialogue about following Jesus and living sent, helping them to shift their construct and begin to live sent. That's one cause and effect example. They heard the story, and it caused them to want to engage, effecting an ongoing relationship where constructs could be shifted, conversation could happen, sending could happen, and coaching could happen.

Another example. At times, when we are already in the midst of relational dialogue, already beginning to see shifting constructs, already deep in conversation, we have found that sharing stories of people living sent is what has the most impact on a person's construct of the idea. In the already developing relationship, the story caused a better understanding of living sent, which caused a greater effect in how they continued to live sent in daily life. Make sense?

Stories do that kind of thing. Think about it. A great movie with a great meaning about a person who lives beyond-self, or at least realizes he or she needs to. How does it make you feel? It causes a lot of emotions and thoughts. At least it does for me and a lot of the people I know.

A short film I saw a couple of years ago has, for example, really challenged me as a dad to four kids. It is the story of a father and son tandem with the last name of Hoyt. It's worth searching for on YouTube if you've not seen it. Talk about living sent to his son. And talk about being transformed and inspired as a father by the joy of your son. The son was born with crippling issues that would prohibit him from ever walking or running. As he grew older, he told his dad, who was not a runner, that he wanted to run in triathlons and marathons. So, in a jogging stroller or whatever it took depending upon the type of event or race it was, they would race together. The video is amazing. Check it out.

All that to say, it inspired me as a dad to not be lazy in being God's love letter to my kids. Living sent to them and to my wife is more important than any other ministry I have as a pastor and as a person. How disingenuous it would be if I focused on living sent to everyone else, but I took my family for granted. If you are a pastor reading this, the same is true for you.

I hope this story challenges you to ask yourself if you minister in spite of your family or if you minister to and with your family. I hope it's the latter, or everything you would be emphasizing to the people you lead would be suspect. That doesn't mean your family is perfect. Don't get wrapped up in that image stuff and put on a show. Be real. It is a crucial way that you can be living sent to the people you lead, if they see the struggles and the victories of your family as you are being a living letter of God's love to them.

Your story matters, too. As do all stories of living sent. So capture them and share them creatively and redundantly.

You get the picture. Remember, it's not just what you teach one Sunday morning that has the greatest effect. It's what you emphasize in every facet of your communication in a consistent, repetitive, creative way.

[CONSIDER and CONVERSE]

*P*rocess through each of these five approaches and evaluate whether your church family's leadership are involved in any of them. Consider how they might become more and more a priority of what you are doing as you hope to cultivate a culture of people living sent.

post scriptum

Contact info:

Jason C. Dukes
email: invitingconversation@gmail.com
blog: www.JasonCDukes.com
book site: www.LiveSent.com
facebook: www.Facebook.com/JasonCDukes
twitter: @JasonCDukes and @LiveSent

Holler at me.

A few resources:

JasonCDukes.com
theWorldWouldNotice.com
ReproducingChurches.com
theChurchofWestOrange.com
theForgottenWays.org
cmaResources.org
TangibleKingdom.com

Follow me on Twitter. My usernames
are @JasonCDukes and @LiveSent.
Connect with me on Facebook at
Facebook.com/JasonCDukes.

Other resources for missional living by
New Hope Publishers

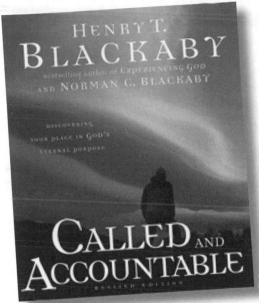

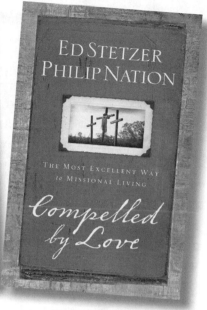

Called and Accountable
Discovering Your Place in God's Eternal Purpose
Henry T. Blackaby and
Norman C. Blackaby
ISBN-10: 1-59669-047-X
ISBN-13: 978-1-59669-047-9

Compelled by Love
The Most Excellent Way to Missional Living
Ed Stetzer and Philip Nation
ISBN-10: 1-59669-227-8
ISBN-13: 978-1-59669-227-5

Beyond Me
*Living a You-First Life
in a Me-First World*
Kathi Macias
ISBN-10: 1-59669-220-0
ISBN-13: 978-1-59669-220-6

Available in bookstores everywhere.

For information about these books or any New Hope product,
visit www.newhopepublishers.com.